T0383846

"This book makes for an excellent read. Ben and Stefan have chosen topics that are unusual and that aren't typically discussed in books of this type. I love Ben's stories and reflections about the experiences he encountered during his stunning climbs. Stefan did a great job in relating Ben's experiences into a theoretical perspective. Finally a book that is entertaining and informative at the same time". – *Peter Schwarzenbauer*, Member of the Board of Management BMW AG. Responsible for: MINI, Rolls-Royce, BMW Motorrad Customer Engagement and Digital Business Innovation BMW Group

"This is an extraordinary book. Boehm reflects on key issues for extreme sports athletes such as uncertainty, fear, suffering, and death. Gröschl relates Boehm's fascinating stories to scholarship relevant for business executives. Those who choose to or must go to extremes will learn a lot from this insightful and unique book". – *Dr Horst Eidenmüller*, a Statutory Professor for Commercial Law at the University of Oxford and a Professorial Fellow of St. Hugh's College, Oxford

"This book is the result of an exciting collaboration between a scholar and extreme sports athlete (who also happens to run a global business). While there are important differences between sports and organizational leadership, there are similarities too, and this book does a good job at foregrounding the best of these. It is a refreshing change from the usual in drawing on Ben's powerful experiences to highlight the challenges of leadership, and innovative strategies for tackling them". – *Mark de Rond*, Professor of Organizational Ethnography at Cambridge University (Judge Business School)

"A book that is entertaining and informative at the same time. I enjoyed how Stefan was able to translate Ben's experiences as leading speed mountaineer into real life business situations. Great to read about topics that give you a totally new look at yourself". – *Dr Thomas Sedran*, CEO of Volkswagen Commercial Vehicles

"One of the most accomplished extreme athletes on the planet, Boehm culls lessons from the life-and-death world of ski-mountaineering and, with the help of scholar Stefan Gröschl, seamlessly applies them to the high-stakes domain of business. From leading teams in extreme conditions to the willingness to embrace failure as a means to spur innovation, Boehm draws from his experiences on the world's most dangerous peaks to elevate what could have been a dense, academic tome into something altogether different: an insightful meditation on business, leadership, and life". – *Kelley McMillan Manley*, freelance journalist and contributor to the *New York Times*

FROM THE DEATH ZONE TO THE BOARDROOM

This book explores experiences and reflections of an extreme sports athlete within the context of classics, the latest scholarly works, and research on topics that are relevant and timely for today's managers and business leaders, and the daily challenges they face.

Conviction, discipline, managing fear in high stakes situations, leading, working with teams, and making decisions in extreme conditions – what will help you in extreme sports can also get you to your goals in business. In *From the Death Zone to the Boardroom*, speed ski mountaineer Benedikt Boehm tells gripping and inspirational stories about his fears, pain, suffering and facing death during his expeditions to some of the world's highest mountains. Throughout, his co-author and professor of leadership and management, Stefan Gröschl integrates scholarly ideas and works beyond traditional business boundaries providing you with unusual insights and thought-provoking alternatives for managing your business.

The combination of extreme athlete, company leader, and business school scholar is unique, and ensures the relevance and timeliness of the selected themes, and the pellucidity of the conceptual context to a readership beyond academic boundaries. The result is advice that is both highly personal and empirically tested; a combination that makes for an absorbing read and unparalleled advice for you and your career.

BENEDIKT BOEHM is CEO of the leading ski touring equipment brand Dynafit and a well-known speed ski mountaineer. Ben has shared his experiences to leading multinational companies and on German national television. He has been featured in national and international journals, newspapers, and television ads.

STEFAN GRÖSCHL is Professor in management at ESSEC Business School. His award-winning writings have been published in numerous books, chapters, and articles in the international trade and academic press. Aside his scholarly works Stefan has a strong interest in long-distance triathlons and apnea diving.

FROM THE DEATH ZONE TO THE BOARDROOM

WHAT BUSINESS LEADERS AND DECISION MAKERS CAN LEARN FROM EXTREME MOUNTAINEERING

Benedikt Boehm and Stefan Gröschl

Routledge
Taylor & Francis Group

LONDON AND NEW YORK

First published 2019
by Routledge
2 Park Square, Milton Park, Abingdon, Oxon OX14 4RN

and by Routledge
52 Vanderbilt Avenue, New York, NY 10017

Routledge is an imprint of the Taylor & Francis Group, an informa business

British Library Cataloguing-in-Publication Data
A catalogue record for this book is available from the British Library

Library of Congress Cataloging-in-Publication Data
Names: Boehm, Benedikt, 1977– author. | Grèoschl, Stefan, author.
Title: From the death zone to the boardroom : what business leaders and decision makers can learn from extreme mountaineering / Benedikt Boehm and Stefan Grèoschl.
Description: 1 Edition. | New York : Routledge, 2019. |
Includes bibliographical references and index. |
Identifiers: LCCN 2019002284 (print) | LCCN 2019021870 (ebook) |
ISBN 9780429442544 (eBook) | ISBN 9781138337251 (hardback : alk. paper) | ISBN 9780429442544 (ebk)
Subjects: LCSH: Leadership. | Decision making.
Classification: LCC HD57.7 (ebook) |
LCC HD57.7 .B635 2019 (print) | DDC 658.4/092—dc23
LC record available at https://lccn.loc.gov/2019002284

ISBN: 978-1-138-33725-1 (hbk)
ISBN: 978-0-429-44254-4 (ebk)

Typeset in Minion Pro
by codeMantra

CONTENTS

CHAPTER ONE

About the book and the authors

SUBTEXT: The interests of a writer and the interests of his readers are never the same and if, on occasion, they happen to coincide, this is a lucky accident[1]

We hope that our book is one of these lucky accidents described by American English poet W.H. Auden, and that you find this book as interesting, informative, and entertaining as we intended it to be. Our book explores Ben's experiences and reflections as an extreme sports athlete within the context of selective scholarly works and research from a wide range of disciplines beyond the general business and management literature.

Over the years, business schools and management scholars have been producing research in insulation from the business world.[2] Many scholars have developed 'knowledge of business rather than for business'.[3] They write in an all-exclusive academic writing style verbosing arguments and complexifying discussions. The turgidities blur what matters to business men and women. Those management ideas which seep through are often short lived due to today's rapidly changing technologies and social developments. One day, strategic thinking gives 'the competitive edge in business',[4] the next day it is all about execution.[5]

In this textbook, we focus on topics and concepts that are independent from technological and social changes. We discuss aspects that matter to every business leader and decision maker. Facing great uncertainties and unpredictability are only some of the commonalities extreme sport athletes and business leaders share, and that are addressed in this book. Our chapters about fear, pain, suffering, and failure introduce themes that are not your 'usual suspects' in business and management textbooks. They provide uncommon insights and alternative perspectives about managing yourself and leading others. They are illustrative and thought-provoking alternatives that challenge traditional business mentalities and business as usual modes.

Each chapter starts with Ben's experiences and reflections from the world of extreme skiing and mountaineering relevant to the chapter's theme. Ben's accounts are at times funny, sad, upsetting, shocking, exciting, or tense. They reflect and illustrate the many ups and downs that come with speed mountaineering in extreme conditions. They are moving and inspiring; and they all have commonalities, parallels, or emblematic and literal connotations to the business world.

Photo 1.1 *Ski touring in the upper glaciers at a height of 6300m on Manaslu (8163m).*

In the second part of each chapter, Stefan puts Ben's experiences and reflections into a business context and makes bisociative connections to businesses and their leaders. Stefan refers to scholarly works from a wide range of disciplines including economics, philosophy, psychology, physiology, and sociology, highlighting their managerial and organizational implications for leaders and decision makers. Despite the complexity of some of the concepts, we have tried to maintain a writing style that is inclusive, pellucid, and to the point.

The combination of extreme athlete, company leader, and business school scholar as our professional backgrounds is unique. We met for the first time in the late 1990s at Oxford Brookes University in England. Ben was a freshman and Stefan was about to finish his PhD. Our paths split when Stefan took on a faculty post in Canada and Ben went to the USA for a student exchange program. In 2013 our paths crossed again after Stefan had read Ben's book about his experiences on Manaslu where an avalanche killed and wounded numerous mountaineers. By then Stefan had increasingly used sport cases as a means to teach management practices and organizational behaviours. And Ben had established himself as a successful keynote speaker presenting his adventures and sharing his experiences in companies across Germany. It did not take much thinking for us to recognize the synergies that could emerge from a joint collaboration.

Our different professional backgrounds ensure the relevance and timeliness of the selected themes, and permit the pellucidity of the conceptual context to a readership beyond academic boundaries. Our different backgrounds also strengthen the bisociative associations between extreme sports, and concepts and ideas framing and shaping human behaviours and organizational practices and processes. Finding parallels and connecting the seemingly different worlds of extreme sports and business makes our book unusual and different to most other textbooks in (extreme) sports and business. Studies that have used mainstream sports data to advance management theory are still embryonic. And although extreme context research is growing and matters, its fragmentation 'risks limiting its potential for advancing management and organization studies.'[6]

Our book can be considered as a starting point and orientation for business men and women wanting to advance their own development and that of their peers and organizations. This is why we address each chapter theme from an individual and organizational perspective. Although many textbooks like to propose a five or ten-steps-to-success fits all approach, we provide detailed endnotes and suggestions for further readings instead, and *takeaways* summing up the key learning points at the end of each chapter. Chapters are written independently from each other, which means that certain terms or scholars are briefly reintroduced.

Following this introduction we start the adventure in Chapter 2 by exploring how to achieve the seemingly unthinkable and how to reach exceptional goals. It is not only a decisive process in extreme adventure performances but one that is also critical for every business man and woman and their career development. In Chapter 3 we discuss how to deal with uncertainty and the unknown. Even though decision makers and organizations operate today in a world that has become increasingly uncertain, most companies and their leaders continue to be hugely unprepared for the unpredictable. In Chapter 4 we explore the many facets and implications of fear of the known and unknown – fear as a warning signal, as a self-analytical tool, and as a motivational method. Chapter 5 addresses a topic against which companies are profoundly biased. We show that failure is an opportunity for personal and professional self-development and growth, for learning and change instead of one of blaming.

Despite the evidence that death awareness is an integral part of the aging process, and despite that there are numerous professions and businesses in which death and mortality play salient roles in the daily routines of their decision makers and employees, organizational scholars have rarely addressed and explored the role of death awareness, death, and mortality in organizational life. In Chapter 6 we make up for this scholarly shortcoming. And similar to the case of mortality, we want to show you some of the positive implications of suffering – our theme for Chapter 7. Whereas organization scholars have largely focused on the negative consequences of mental and physical suffering at the workplace, we show how suffering for a particular goal and reason can positively influence your willpower, self-control, and state of mind. In Chapter 8 we expand the understanding of leadership and decision making in extreme conditions and contexts. Much has been written about leadership and decision making in a general business and management context, however, in extreme conditions such as the death zone the two topics start to show very different dynamics. So far, however, within the leadership field, leadership in extreme contexts has been one of the least researched areas, whereas decision making under extreme conditions has been predominantly discussed in specialized fields such as the military.

In our final chapter we explore speed and lightness. As has been the case for many of the themes that we address throughout this book, there are only few management and organization studies, texts, or concepts which have addressed lightness and speed in the conventional sense or in the way described by Ben in the context of mountaineering. This came as a surprise to us; and we hope we can show you why in Chapter 9. The final chapter is about Ben. In times in which work life balance is on everybody's mind, Stefan felt that Ben should share how he manages to train and prepare for an 8000m speed ascent, run a global business, and have a family with three little kids and a wife at the same time. Of course this last Chapter 10 also addresses some other key issues that are on many business men and women's minds including topics such as sustainability and responsible leadership. Enjoy the book, and may this become one of Auden's lucky accidents.

Photo 1.2 *Working dinner at Ben's place in Munich*

NOTES

1 *Reading* –An essay by W. H. Auden.

2 Bouchikhi, H. and Kimberly, J. 2015. Soapbox: Why business schools are running in place? *Financial Times*. At http://www.ft.com/cms/s/2/2707b720-2007-11e5-ab0f-6bb9974f25d0.html#axzz3iVtkIxwk.

3 Starkey, K. and Stempest, N. 2008. A clear sense of purpose? The evolving role of the business school. *Journal of Management Development*, 27(4), 379.

4 Dixit, A. and Nalebuff, B. 1991. *Thinking strategically*. New York: W.W. Norton & Company.

5 Interview with Carlos Ghosn, CEO of Renault-Nissan at Stanford Business School. 2014. Carlos Ghosn: Five percent of the challenge is the strategy. Ninety-five percent is the execution. At https://www.gsb.stanford.edu/insights/carlos-ghosn-five-percent-challenge-strategy-ninety-five-percent-execution

6 Hannah, S., Uhl-Bien, M. Avolio, B. and Cavarretta, F. 2009. A framework for examining leadership in extreme contexts. *The Leadership Quarterly*, 20, 897–919.

CHAPTER TWO
About the unthinkable

SUBTEXT: To realize your unthinkable goals you have to set yourself unthinkable goals

On August 4, 2006, at 12:31pm an unthinkable goal of mine came true. I ski mountaineered my first 8000m mountain, Gasherbrum 2, at 8035m. Ski mountaineering is a skiing discipline in which you climb the mountain either on skis with removable climbing skins or when too steep by carrying the skis, and then ski down. Together with my friend Sebastian 'Basti' Haag we speed climbed Gasherbrum 2 in 12.5 hours and then skied back down to advanced Basecamp (ABC). Neither when I started cross country skiing in 1988 as an 11-year-old boy, nor as a ski touring athlete in my early 20s did I imagine to speed climb and stand up on an 8000m mountain peak one day.

It was not until the ski mountaineering world championship in 2004 in Vall d'Aran, Spain, and during my races at the famous 'Patrouille des Glaciers',[1] that I discovered my true passion for expeditions and for shifting the methodology of ski mountaineering racing into higher altitudes. It was also during that time that I started to play with the idea of speed climbing 8000m mountains and to ski down from their peaks. For me speed ski mountaineering 8000m peaks was the ultimate challenge – not only from a physical or athletic perspective. Skiing down from a mountain like Gasherbrum 2 would also take a lot of mental strength. I knew that the mountain's steepness and deepness made the climb, and in particular the skiing down, a very risky business. One mistake on your skis and it would be over. This physical and mental challenge created an immense pressure but also motivation; it set into motion a flywheel within me which would push me through all those years of preparation and training.

Most of my 'missions impossible' and goals in those days and even today have been team efforts. Setting impossible or unthinkable goals such as speed climbing Gasherbrum 2 or Manaslu (8163m) are often explored with my climbing and expedition buddies. In these discussions, plans for expedition and touring projects regularly start out as ambitious but doable. The diverse skill sets, competencies, and experiences amongst the team members, however, have often led us to push the boundaries to the extreme whereby the final goal becomes somewhat unthinkable. For the Gasherbrum 2 and Manaslu expeditions, for example, it was Basti who pushed us to downhill ski the mountains from their peaks. As Basti was a much better downhill skier than me, his ambitions and goals in terms of downhill skiing were far greater than mine. He was able to downhill ski mountains which seemed impossible to me. In many ski mountaineering projects I would have never aimed that high in terms of downhill skiing without Basti's drive and encouragement. In contrast, I was the stronger climber and my athletic mountaineering goals were higher than what Basti imagined could be done; for example, climbing Manaslu (8163m) directly from Basecamp in 15 hours. Put together, we created a symbiosis of sub goals which were thought achievable individually (by at least one of us) yet considered impossible or unachievable when viewed as a whole.

This goal setting process of impossible or unthinkable ideas illustrates how my projects emerged from within me and my mountaineering friends. Rarely did I accept a project or goals that were imposed on me externally. Though there have always been external parties such as film production companies, sport products companies, and others who have approached me with some crazy ideas, if I am not positive about their goals and ideas, if I cannot tailor their proposals toward what I believe in, then it does not work out for me. On the other hand, I often found inspiration from outside. I paid special attention to 'exotic' stories. Stories of high-altitude adventures where my idea of transferring the ski touring racing style might work. I also had to watch out for and catch the right opportunities. For example, finding people I could trust and who organized and/or guided expeditions at an affordable price. I was searching and actively working for enablers that could get me closer to my goals.

Aside from the importance of my ski mountaineering friends and partners in coming up with seemingly impossible goals and objectives, is the sense of self-confidence; a self-confidence which has been nourished over years by the achievement of subgoals. Setting subgoals with the right balance – ambitious and yet achievable – has always been critical in my pursuit of seemingly impossible missions such as Gasherbrum 2. We did not speed climb this mountain at 8035m without having slowly worked our way up training and speed climbing on numerous mountains between 4000–7000m. It took a lot of patience and willpower. Per year we did around 300–400,000 altitude meters – two-thirds on skis and the other third on foot or mountain bike. One of our regular training routines early on, in 2004, was the crossing of seven 4000m mountain peaks in one day at the Monte Rosa in the Pennine

Alps. And there were times when I got up every second or third night at 3am to climb and run up to the Alpspitze (my main training mountain right next to the highest peak in Germany called Zugspitze) in 2600m altitude.

I am often asked if I never need a break from such intense training sessions or periods. Paradoxically, it is these training sessions that relax me. They are my form of meditation, my break from the daily routines and everyday life. Running or skiing up a mountain at 4am when everybody else sleeps is often the only time when I can mentally completely switch off. No laptop, no cellphone. No connectivity with the outside world – the only connection is with me. Pure flow of movement of my skies. Flow of thoughts. Moving like in trance. All is fluid and connected as one. It is these moments when I have the best ideas, when I can think creatively. My pencil and my paper pad are always waiting in the car.

In 2004 I also climbed and skied with Basti and another friend our first 6000m mountains in the Peruvian Andes. In those early days of trying to ski mountaineer at higher altitude we did everything one should avoid doing – from not acclimatizing to choosing the wrong equipment. The same day we arrived in Huaraz, the starting point for all tours to the 33 6000m peaks in the Peruvian Cordillera Blanca, we started our climbing tour. With more than 30kg of luggage each, hardly any drinking water, and no step by step acclimation, we speed hiked to our Basecamp at 4400m into the Ishinca Valley and continued to the Urus at 5495m. Back at Basecamp 3 hours later, the three of us had to coop-up in a two-man tent and got stuck with some cold food. All our bottles for our portable gasoline cooker had been filled by our Peruvian friend from the gas station with diesel. Basti ended up with a pulmonary edema in the middle of the night, and we decided to head back to Huaraz. So much for our first 6000m peak attempt in the Peruvian Cordillera Blanca.

Our Peruvian experience made us learn the hard way that our idea of applying ski mountaineering techniques to high altitudes is somewhat more complex than we thought. Our reflections helped us to make some significant changes for our subsequent expeditions – from taking more time to acclimatize to being better equipped. In 2005 I made my first serious speed climb ascent in high altitude with Basti and our friend Mathias Robl. With two liters of water and 15 energy gels in my front pocket – and no down suit or tent – we climbed Mustagh Ata (7546m) in Western China in 9 hours and 25 min and skied back to Basecamp in another hour. Even though our expedition was a success and we all arrived back home safe and healthy with a record ascent of Mustagh Ata, we critically analyzed every single aspect of our expedition. Such a critical analysis after every failed and successful expedition or tour became an important process in getting me closer to any of my unthinkable goals. The experiences and reflections helped me to continuously correct, adjust, and perfect my techniques and equipment for my speed climbing projects in high altitude. But more importantly they strengthened my self-confidence. Without this strong belief in myself and my mental strength any ascent in high altitude and very low levels of oxygen is doomed to fail. There comes a point when the physical capabilities are exhausted and the physical suffering can only be overcome with a very strong mind and mental toughness. Without this absolute will the unthinkable remains impossible.

My mind has also always played another important role when reaching for the unthinkable. Getting closer to this goal means visualizing the goal and all its details. For my first 8000m mountain I started visualizing every step and every second from the Basecamp to the top about two years beforehand. Every move was in my mind and drawn on a mind map. I knew exactly where I had to be on that mountain at what time. I collected all the information I could get about this mountain. I studied every satellite picture. I spoke to every person who I knew and who had climbed Gasherbrum 2. The more I visualized, the more info I collected, the less unthinkable became this unthinkable goal.

With this visualizing and data collection process I explored every possible obstacle, and identified every skill and equipment needed to overcome these barriers. I had to go in new and different ways to reach my seemingly impossible goals. Methods and techniques that worked in ski tours and races at low altitude no longer worked in low oxygen environments. Being fast at 8000m is about going slow but steady and keeping a consistent and technically perfect flow. Trying to compete with others or to rush can be deadly. These new ways meant creativity and courage. Creativity to find innovative tools and gears that adapted to the adversities in high altitude, and courage to go in new ways and do things differently.

In 2006 I felt ready to go. Basti and I were hungry for Gasherbrum 2. Despite the many setbacks and failures on the way we never questioned our ultimate, unthinkable goal. It was clear to us that with all the training we put in, all the motivation we had, and all the learnings and corrections over the years from our other expeditions, we were as prepared as we could be. We knew we might be able to make it. But of course, we also realized that not everything depended on us – the weather, and other uncertainties for which we could not control had to be anticipated – but more about this in the next chapter.

Photo 2.1 *Ben reaching the summit of Manaslu (8163m) in a non-stop push directly from Basecamp (4900m) in a world record time of 15 hours at 9.00am, September 31, 2012. No hands in the air and no signs of victory. The days prior the summit push had been a mental and physical rollercoaster. Only, a week before the speed ascent, on September 23, Ben and his five team members had been witnesses to of one of the most deadly avalanches in the Himalayas. The avalanche killed 11 climbers in Camp 3 right next to Ben's team camp spot. Ben and his friends were the first to arrive at the avalanche battlefield only 20 minutes after the avalanche. They were searching for survivors and treating them for 6 hours before the helicopters came.*

Photo 2.2 *When the weather conditions allowed it, this was our view out of the tent from Manaslu Basecamp (4900m).*

GOAL SETTING

For Ben, individual goal setting has been a decisive process in his extreme adventure performances and achievements. Research on individual goal setting has its roots in organizational theory with a strong focus on effort, persistence, and task performance. The relevance and benefits of goal setting for organizations and their employees' motivation and engagement have been reported in numerous studies.[2] Motivational theorists such as Herzberg,[3] Maslow,[4] Alderfer,[5] and McClelland,[6] who studied what people needed in the workplace to be motivated, and Vroom,[7] Porter and Lawler,[8] and Pinder,[9] who explored the cognitive processes and relationships in employees' motivation, have all highlighted the importance of goal setting for employees' motivation, engagement, and commitment.

DIFFICULTY AND DETAILS

Ben's case illustrates how countless training hours of physical and mental preparation continuously put in over many years have helped him to achieve seemingly unthinkable goals – from speed climbing and skiing down 8000m mountains to speed crossing multiple high altitude peaks with skis and mountain bikes. Researchers have shown that 'people exert more effort and work more persistently to attain difficult goals than they do when they attempt to attain less difficult goals'.[10] This is particularly the case for goals that are intrinsically driven and which are based on autotelic[11] experiences – experiences in which the activities are their very own goals and rewards, and which are 'done for their own sake'.[12]

Traditionally, studies about goal setting and task performance have focused on task complexity and on how detailed the goals are. One of the key arguments that has emerged from these studies is that people who work toward specific and difficult goals outperform those who work with vague or abstract instructions.[13] As Steven Kotler explains, 'clarity gives us certainty. We know what to do and we know where to focus our attention while doing it. When goals are clear, metacognition[14] is replaced by in-the-moment cognition'.[15] An illustration of this in-the-moment focus and attention is Daniel Simons and Christopher Chabris' psychology experiment 'The invisible gorilla' at Harvard University in the late 1990s.[16] Simons and Chabris asked people to watch a video in which several Harvard students would pass a basketball to each other in a circle. In the middle of the video clip a student dressed as a gorilla could be seen for 5 seconds crossing the circle. Viewers of the video were asked before the start of the video to count how often the ball was thrown between the students. When asked about the gorilla after the video clip, half of the viewers explained they have missed the gorilla walking through the circle. According to Kotler 'when the brain is charged with a clear goal, focus narrows considerably, the unimportant is disregarded, the now is all that's left'.[17]

VISUALIZATION

Ben's account of how he planned each stage in his preparation over many years, and the minutious visualization process of each step of his first ascent of an 8000m mountain is exemplary of how long and detailed the preparation process can be when wanting to achieve such difficult and complex goals. Famous South Tyrolian mountaineer Reinhold Messner was 'six years pregnant' with his idea of climbing Mount Everest (8848m) without oxygen before he did so with Peter Habeler in May 1978.[18] US-born free solo rock climber[19] Alex Honnold achieved in 2017 the 'moon-landing of free soloing' by climbing rope-free the 1000m El Capitan wall in Yosemite Park in the USA in 4 hours[20]. Honnold describes this achievement his biggest life goal for which he prepared himself intensively for more than 4 years. Similar to Ben, Alex visualized, rehearsed, and memorized every single grip and step along the wall.[21] After numerous climbs with ropes of every section of the route, 'a lot of the handholds felt like old friends'[22] and the climb 'was like executing a routine'.[23]

Visualizing and outlining detailed descriptions of each stage, and defining clear subgoals has kept Ben, Reinhold Messner, and Alex Honnold on track, confirmed their progress, which in turn increased their confidence and self-efficacy – or as big wave surf legend Laird Hamilton explains: 'You set up challenges that are more than what you've ever did before. And by getting through it, you get the sensation you've completed something. And if it's dangerous, then other things that scare you, the experience will strengthen you for those situations'.[24] An ambiguous 'trying your best' approach would not have pushed these athletes hard enough to put in the necessary time and effort over so many years to reach their goals.

SUBGOALS

Setting clear goals combined with subgoals that indicate progress and encourage persistence does not only work for extreme athletes. The power of progress has been considered fundamental to human nature – even though 'only few managers understand it or know how to leverage progress to boost motivation' of their employees.[25] Studies show that the majority of managers continue to rank recognition of good work as their top motivator and put progress last on their list.[26] The problem is, however, without achievement what's there to recognize? Creating a sense of progress can be achieved by setting minor milestones, and detailed and meaningful goals. Even ordinary, incremental progress can increase people's engagement in their work and their happiness.[27]

LEARNING GOALS

Setting difficult and detailed goals, however, does not necessarily ensure higher task performance. Studies have shown that setting challenging goals and tasks for which only 'minimal prior learning or performance routines exist, where strategies that were effective suddenly cease to be so', can be counterproductive to the task performance.[28] Such cases require the development of new abilities and skills rather than an increase of effort or persistence. Therefore, it is setting specific and difficult learning goals instead of challenging and complex performance goals that will lead to higher performance in situations with limited known methods and procedures and/or ineffective strategies.[29]

As Ben admits, he learnt the hard way; his preparation for his first 8000m mountain with his traditional touring and ski climbing techniques and strategies, which functioned well at low altitude levels, would make him fail when applied in low oxygen environments. During their Peru tour in 2004, their narrow focus on climbing as many 6000m peaks as possible in the shortest amount of time created a tunnel vision amongst Ben and his mountaineering buddies. Their focus on a performance outcome goal distracted Ben and his peers' attention from the exploration of new task relevant strategies and the learning of different task relevant techniques.[30] With the analysis of his Peru failure, Ben realized that he had to unlearn some of his 'old ways of doing things' and acquire new techniques that had to be continuously corrected, adjusted, and perfected for his speed climbing projects in high altitude. He started to shift his focus from being less results oriented to more process oriented. In China and during his training back home his learning goals took over from some of the performance goals. According to Gerard Seijts and his colleagues a

> learning goal shifts attention to the discovery and implementation of task-relevant strategies or procedures and away from task outcome achievement. This is because tasks that are novel or complex for an individual often require attentional resources for learning what is required in order to perform them well.[31]

By alternating performance goals and learning goals during the different stages, goal setting was no longer 'just' an enabler of Ben's motivation but an equally critical factor in the development of new abilities required to achieve his big goals.

GOAL ATTAINMENT

SELF-EFFICACY

By focusing on learning goals during the different preparation stages and later expeditions, Ben's self-efficacy increased – or as he put it, every failed and successful expedition and tour strengthened his self-confidence. The notion of self-efficacy has its roots in social cognitive theory. Scholars such as psychologist Albert Bandura have defined self-efficacy as one's belief in one's ability to succeed in specific situations or accomplish a task.[32] Learning new skills and abilities, achieving challenging learning goals, and having positive performance experiences increase self-efficacy[33] – like in the case of Ben. Other aspects that have been identified as affecting self-efficacy include verbal persuasion and vicarious experiences.[34] Ben often worked in small teams for and during his mountaineering expeditions where persuasion in form of peer-encouragement and vicarious experiences in form of performance comparisons and evaluations amongst the team members further increased the self-efficacy of Ben and his mountaineering partners.

Studies have shown that individuals with high self-efficacy are engaged in activities and in the pursuit of their goals to a greater extent, with greater self-determination and with greater persistence than those with low self-efficacy.[35] Ben's absolute will and belief in himself played an important part in his quests – especially in very high-altitude situations. According to Messner, 'in those situations the will is the decisive engine – without it you won't make a single move anymore and you just mutate into a zombie'.[36]

FLOW

Other critical parts in the goal attainment process that have been identified by social cognitive theorists include self-evaluation,[37] self-observation,[38] and self-reaction[39] – or as Ben's experiences have illustrated, continuously analyzing, reflecting, correcting, adjusting, and perfecting. Although these different cognitive elements are seemingly separate processes, Ben describes situations in which they all merge into one. In these situations, Ben's state of mind is in a flow – his attention is reduced to the activity of the very moment. When Ben is in a flow, when he skis up the mountain, his concentration is completely absorbed by his skiing. According to psychologist Mihaly Csikszentmihalyi in such a flow state

> one of the most universal and distinctive features of optimal experiences takes place: people become so involved in what they are doing that the activity becomes spontaneous, almost automatic, they stop being aware of themselves as separate from the actions they are performing.[40]

Reflection, analysis, feedback, and (re)action are fluid and immediate as any delay through a separation of these cognitive processes can be deadly when speed climbing on 8000m peaks or free soloing rocks and walls.

The notion of flow that Ben has been experiencing in his trainings and expeditions, and that was conceptualized by Csikszentmihalyi in the

1990s, has been reintroduced by Steven Kotler in 2014 studying how extreme athletes use flow to achieve their seemingly impossible goals.[41] According to Kotler, flow 'is an optimal state of consciousness, a peak state where we both feel our best and perform our best'.[42] Within the business world, however, only 'few business leaders have mastered the skill of generating it reliably in the workplace'.[43]

While Steven Kotler's works on the notion of flow have created a media hype about seemingly impossible individual performances and achievements, the general management literature and the business press have been focusing on impossible goals at an organizational level – from Mayer's promise to bring Yahoo back to greatness, to Elon Musk's production and sales projections of his Teslas, and Walmarts' renewable energy predictions.[44] Yet, as much as these organizations and their leaders have failed to achieve their proclaimed goals, 'most organizations have no idea as to how to manage specific challenging goals'.[45]

STRETCH GOALS

Management scholars have described such impossible or challenging organizational objectives as stretch goals. A stretch goal is defined as 'an organizational goal with an objective probability of attainment that may be unknown but is seemingly impossible given current capabilities', and characterized by its 'extreme difficulty' and its 'extreme novelty'.[46] Despite the business media's particular interest in organizational stretch goals, academic studies have largely been limited to general commentaries and applied case studies.[47] Sitkin and his colleagues' critical and acclaimed analysis of stretch goals and their impact on organizational learning and performance remains the exception.[48] In their study and in a recent *Harvard Business Review* article,[49] Sitkin and his colleagues predict the impact of stretch goals by recent organizational performance and the availability of excess uncommitted financial and other resources (slack resources). The authors argue that in organizations which have recently performed well and which have readily available extra, unused resources, employees are more likely to buy into extremely challenging goals than employees of companies which have recently been troubled and which experience resource constraints.[50]

In reality, however, companies with strong recent performance and extra, unused resources – those which are in the best position to go for the impossible – avoid stretch goals because their success has made them risk-adverse and complacent. Instead, it is troubled companies with resource constraints which become extremely risk seeking and which push themselves toward the unthinkable. When

> organizations pursue stretch goals as a way of overcoming recent failure ("going for broke") while ignoring their tight resource constraints, they're asking for trouble. They should resist the temptation to "fly to the sun," because their patched-together efforts are most likely doomed.[51]

The following are key arguments and 'takeaways' that derived from the individual and organizational goal setting and goal attainment literature.

KEY ARGUMENTS AND TAKEAWAYS:

- Attain difficult goals when you have the relevant skills and abilities. This way you exert more effort and work more persistently than when you attempt to attain less difficult goals.
- Work toward specific and difficult goals when you have the relevant skills and abilities. This way you are performing better than when working with vague or abstract instructions.
- Create detailed and meaningful goals. These are critical for your progress. Any sense of progress can increase your engagement in your work and your feeling of happiness.
- Focus on specific and difficult learning goals when facing situations where there are limited known methods and procedures and/or ineffective strategies. Challenging and complex performance goals in such situations will be less effective.

- Increase your self-efficacy. With high self-efficacy you engage in activities and in the pursuit of your goals to a greater extent, with greater self-determination, and with greater persistence than with low self-efficacy
- In organizations which have recently performed well and which have readily available slack resources, employees are most likely to buy into extremely challenging goals.
- In organizations which have recently been troubled and which experience resource constraints, employees are least likely to buy into extremely challenging goals.

NOTES

1 A legendary ski mountaineering race organized every two years by the Swiss Army, in which military and civilian teams compete.

2 Locke, E. and Latham, G. 2002. Building a practically useful theory of goal setting and task motivation: A 35-year odyssey. *American Psychologist*, 57, 705–717.

3 Herzberg, F. 1968. One more time: How do you motivate employees? *Harvard Business Review*, 46, 53–62.

4 Maslow, A. 1970. *Motivation and personality*. Reading, MA: Addison-Wesley.

5 Alderfer, C. 1972. *Existence, relatedness, and growth*. New York: Free Press.

6 McClelland, D. 1976. *The achieving society*. New York: Irvington Publishers.

7 Vroom, V.1964. *Work and motivation*. San Francisco, CA: Jossey-Bass.

8 Porter, L. and Lawler, E. (1968). *Managerial attitudes and performance*. New York: McGraw-Hill.

9 Pinder, C. 1987. Valence-instrumentality-expectancy theory. In R. M. Steers and L. W. Porter (Eds.), *Motivation and work behavior* (4th ed.) (pp. 69–89). New York: McGraw-Hill.

10 Schweitzer, M., Ordonez, L. and Douma, B. 2004. Goal setting as a motivator of unethical behavior. *Academy of Management Journal*, 47(3), 422–432 (page 422).

11 Autotelic derives from the Greek words 'auto' (self) and 'telos' (goal).

12 Kotler, S. 2014. *The rise of superman*. New York: HarperCollins.

13 Locke, E. and Latham, G. 2002. Building a practically useful theory of goal setting and task motivation: A 35-year odyssey. *American Psychologist*, 57, 705–717.

14 Thinking about thinking: Reflecting on our own thinking process by, for example, evaluating what we think about a situation or wondering how we could have been mistaken in a belief (see Nolen-Hoeksema, S., Fredrickson, B., Loftus, G. and Wagenaar, W. 2009. *Atkinson and Hilgard's introduction to psychology*. Andover, UK: Cengage Learning.

15 Kotler, S. 2014. *The rise of superman*. New York: HarperCollins.

16 For more details about the experiment and the video go to http://www.the invisiblegorilla.com/gorilla_experiment.html

17 Kotler, S. 2014. *The rise of superman*. New York: HarperCollins.

18 Interview of Johanna Stöckl with Reinhold Messner in Klettern, 08/05/2018.

19 Climbing in the free solo style means Alex ascends without a rope or protective equipment of any kind.

20 Quoting Tommy Caldwell in Synnott, M. 2017. Exclusive: Climber completes the most dangerous rope-free ascent ever. *National Geographic*, June 3. At https://www.nationalgeographic.com/adventure/features/athletes/alex-honnold/most-dangerous-free-solo-climb-yosemite-national-park-el-capitan/

21 Interviews with *National Geographic*'s Mark Synnott (https://www.national geographic.com/adventure/features/athletes/alex-honnold/interview-rope-free-solo-climb-yosemite-el-capitan/) and with talkshow host Jimmy Kimmel (https://www.climbing.com/videos/watch-alex-honnold-on-jimmy-kimmel-live/)

22 Interview with *National Geographic*'s Mark Synnott (https://www.national geographic.com/adventure/features/athletes/alex-honnold/interview-rope-free-solo-climb-yosemite-el-capitan/)

23 Interview with talkshow host Jimmy Kimmel (https://www.climbing.com/videos/watch-alex-honnold-on-jimmy-kimmel-live/)

24 Laird Hamilton in Kotler, S. 2014. *The rise of superman*. New York: HarperCollins (page 41).

25 Amabile, T. and Kramer, S. 2011. The power of small wins. *Harvard Business Review*, May, 71–80 (page 72).

26 Amabile, T. and Kramer, S. 2011. The power of small wins. *Harvard Business Review*, May, 71–80.

27 Amabile, T. and Kramer, S. 2011. The power of small wins. *Harvard Business Review*, May, 71–80 (page 75).

28 Seijts, G., Latham, G., Tasa, K. and Latham, B. 2004. Goal setting and goal orientation: An integration of two different yet related literatures. *Academy of Management Journal*, 47(2), 227–239 (page 235).

29 Seijts, G. and Latham, G. 2005. Learning versus performance goals: When should each be used? *Academy of Management Executive*, 19(1), 124–131.

30 Locke, E. and Latham, G. 2006. New directions in goal setting theory. *Association for Psychological Science*, 15(5), 265–268.

31 Seijts, G., Latham, G., Tasa, K. and Latham, B. 2004. Goal setting and goal orientation: An integration of two different yet related literatures. *Academy of Management Journal*, 47(2), 227–239 (page 229).

32 Bandura, A. 1977. *Social learning theory*. Englewood Cliffs, NJ: Prentice-Hall.

33 Bandura, A. 1997. *Self-efficacy: The exercise of control*. New York: Freeman.

34 Redmond, B. 2010. *Self-efficacy theory: Do I think that I can succeed in my work? Work attitudes and motivation*. The Pennsylvania State University; World Campus; Bandura, A. 1997. *Self-efficacy: The exercise of control*. New York: Freeman.

35 Deci, E. and Ryan, R. 2000. The 'what' and 'why' of goal pursuits: Human needs and the self-determination of behavior. *Psychological Inquiry*, 11, 227–268; Bandura, A. 1986. *Social foundations of thought and action: A social cognitive theory*. Englewood Cliffs, NJ: Prentice-Hall.

36 Interview of Johanna Stöckl with Reinhold Messner in Klettern, 08/05/2018.

37 Bandura, A. 1991. Social cognitive theory of self-regulation. *Organizational Behavior and Human Decision Processes*, 50, 248–287.

38 Zimmerman, B. and Schunk, D. 2001. *Self-regulated learning and academic achievement*. Mahwah, NJ: Lawrence Erlbaum Associates, Inc.

39 Bandura, A. 1997. *Self-efficacy: The exercise of control*. New York: Freeman.

40 Csikszentmihalyi, M. 1990. *Flow: The psychology of optimal experience*. New York: HarperCollins Publishers (page 53).

41 Kotler, S. and Wheal, J. 2017. *Stealing fire*. New York: HarperCollins; Kotler, S. 2014. *The rise of superman*. New York: HarperCollins.

42 Kotler, S. 2014. *The rise of superman*. New York: HarperCollins (page iii).

43 Cranston, S. and Keller, S. 2013. Increasing the meaning quotient of work. *McKinsey*, January, 1–12 (page 4).

44 See Sitkin, S., Miller, C. and See, K. 2017. The stretch goal paradox. *Harvard Business Review*, January–February, 92–99.

45 Seijts, G. and Latham, G. 2005. Learning versus performance goals: When should each be used? *Academy of Management Executive*, 19(1), 124–131 (page 124).

46 Sitkin, S., Miller, C., See, K., Lawless, M. and Carton, A. 2011. The paradox of stretch goals: Organizations in pursuit of the seemingly impossible. *Academy of Management Review*, 36(3), 544–566 (page 547).

47 Sitkin, S., Miller, C., See, K., Lawless, M. and Carton, A. 2011. The paradox of stretch goals: Organizations in pursuit of the seemingly impossible. *Academy of Management Review*, 36(3), 544–566.

48 Sitkin, S., Miller, C., See, K., Lawless, M. and Carton, A. 2011. The paradox of stretch goals: Organizations in pursuit of the seemingly impossible. *Academy of Management Review*, 36(3), 544–566.

49 Sitkin, S., Miller, C. and See, K. 2017. The stretch goal paradox. *Harvard Business Review*, January–February, 92–99.

50 Sitkin, S., Miller, C. and See, K., Lawless, M. and Carton, A. 2011. The paradox of stretch goals: Organizations in pursuit of the seemingly impossible. *Academy of Management Review*, 36(3), 544–566.

51 Sitkin, S., Miller, C. and See, K. 2017. The stretch goal paradox. *Harvard Business Review*, January–February, 92–99 (page 97).

CHAPTER THREE

About uncertainty

SUBTEXT: Expect the unexpected

NOTE: For this chapter we are grateful to the contributions and co-authorship of Jan Lepoutre[1]

Whenever I started an expedition or a tour with my climbing buddies there was always an uncertainty – an uncertainty if we make it to the top, an uncertainty about what we are going to face up there, and the uncertainty if we make it back alive or in one piece. With those uncertainties on our minds we created a lot of our own pressures and tensions, and an atmosphere of anxiety. Most farewell parties before tours and expeditions were rather small and brief as in the back of everybody's mind was the thought whether or not one will make it back.

When it comes to the uncertainties during my expeditions, I always differentiated between what I call the known unknowns and the complete unknowns. The latter were the completely unexpected challenges – those which you just cannot anticipate or prepare for. As much as I can train and prepare for an 8000m peak by climbing in the Peruvian Andes or Mustagh Ata at 7546m, I still don't know what it would feel like to speed climb another 500–600m higher at that altitude to make it to Gasherbrum 2 at 8035m or Manaslu at 8163m. I could not simulate these 500m in my training – I had to experience them with all their completely unknowns. Or during my ascent on Mustagh Ata in 2007, when we found two frozen bodies at 7300m – the woman already dead, the man still alive. You are suddenly confronted with something that you just do not expect. You cannot prepare for such a situation mentally or physically.

For such situations which are completely unknown and unforeseeable, I have to develop a certain lightness – otherwise the anxiety and pressure before and during a tour will be too overwhelming and destructive. Only my experiences can get me to this lightness and calmness. The more I experience and overcome completely unexpected situations the more confidence in myself I develop – confidence in my technical skills and competencies, but even more importantly, confidence in my ability to recognize and respect my limits. In 2009 we turned around on our ascent of Broad Peak 20 altitude meters below the peak after 18 hours of climbing. We had set ourselves beforehand the time limit of 18 hours to reach the top to limit the risks for our descent. It was a tough decision but one which had to be made to make it back safely. Having the lightness and coolness to turn around before reaching a peak or goal has saved my life more than once.

Knowing and accepting the completely unknown as a type of uncertainty for which you cannot prepare and control, and which you can only manage in the very situation, requires what I call 'situational' decision making (see also Chapter 8). For example, when I was solo climbing Manaslu, at 7400m I faced suddenly lots of extremely icy winds. This was totally unexpected at the time – there were no winds at all during the days before. I could not continue upwards. But if I turned around and went back down, I would not have had the energy for another attempt to ascend the peak. I remembered that somewhere around this altitude there must be the official Camp 4. I decided to look for a tent to stay in until sunrise and to wait for the wind to hopefully calm down. It turned out that it was the right decision in that situation. At first light the winds calmed down and I made it to the peak. But I must admit it was one of the coldest nights I have ever experienced.

Uncertainties that I described earlier as known unknowns can also be extreme winds – but in these cases these would be expected in the situations into which I am getting. Just like the steep passages or crevasses that I would anticipate on my ascents. These are the known aspects. What remains unknown is how steep or icy the different passages will be, or how deep and wide the crevasses might be on our ascents. For such situations you can train and prepare. As I explained in the previous chapter, the approach that my climbing partners and I have always chosen is gradual exposure toward the known unknowns that we would be facing on our tours and expeditions. Before I speed climbed Manaslu in 2012, my climbing partners and I ascended the mountain continuously up and down the traditional way until 7000m – camp by camp – the weeks before. We did this mainly to acclimatize and prepare our bodies but also to get to know and get used to the route and the challenges we had to overcome for the summit push. The summit region beyond 7000m remained uncertain.

As with every tour, it was about increasing the known parts and reducing the unknown aspects and hence minimizing the risks. None of my climbing buddies nor I longs for death or is an adrenaline junkie. I have three small kids and a wife to whom I always want to come back alive and in one piece. Having said that, I believe that it is only the risks and the different uncertainties that come with my expeditions and tours that open up new opportunities. Only when I leave my comfort zone and its certainties will I be able to grow and develop. I turned the extremely steep downhill skiing challenge at Gasherbrum into an opportunity. In my preparation for Gasherbrum 2 I selected training mountains and downhill tours in my region, in Chamonix and in the Karwendel that all continuously increased in steepness. By skiing these steeper and steeper mountains I trained and perfected my technique and the movement routines essential for Gasherbrum 2. At the end of the preparation phase there was not much thinking involved anymore in my downhill skiing, every move flew and was somewhat automated and intuitive. Routines and intuition are absolutely critical to me when I have to make fast decisions – in particular when I face unknown situations in high altitude. I cannot sit down and go through the different options and alternatives at 8000m where hypothermia kicks in within minutes, and where every thought costs oxygen – of which there is only very little at that altitude. In many cases I have no rational explanation for my decision in the very moment I take it; it just feels the right thing to do.

But the routines and automation that I developed do not mean, however, that I could ski down Gasherbrum 2 with closed eyes. On the contrary – the ski descent required a great deal of attentiveness and focus. All my concentration is in that very moment. In any of such situations of great uncertainty, I need to be able to recall routines and automated movement sequences and the same time be fully alert and concentrated.

When this duality of somewhat contradicting states of mind is missing, accidents happen – and in many cases they are fatal. When we go into an uncertainty we are fully focused and concentrated – our environmental scanning is switched on permanently. In seemingly easier, not so challenging situations we are not always fully concentrated, and it is often then that the accidents happen – in mountaineering but also in many other sports such as in the cases of Thomas Huber and Natalia Molchanova. Thomas is a well-known German rock climber who plummeted 16m during a relatively easy ascent at the Brendlberg suffering severe injuries. He admitted afterwards that he had been too lax and did not pay enough attention.[2] Natalia was a record holder and world champion who dominated the extreme sport of free diving for many years. She could hold her breath more than nine minutes and dive to a depth of more than 125m; yet she died on a recreational 'just for fun' dive in 2015.[3]

Sometimes it is also just a question of being lucky; of being at the right place at the right time, or vice versa – being at the wrong place at the wrong time. In particular in my early days as a speed mountaineer I had more luck than brains. I was a dare devil who put himself into risks into which I would never put myself today. And worse, at the time I did not even realize what risks I was putting myself in. Only now after having seen what can happen in a split second of inattentiveness and recklessness, and the amount of fatal accidents I have come across during my expeditions, am I much more cautious and aware before and in complete unknown situations.

Photo 3.1 *Making our way crossing the glaciers of Manaslu (8163m). After many days of bad weather we didn't care anymore and just went up to Camp 1 every day for a workout.*

Photo 3.2 *The famous ice falls of Manaslu (8163m) not only challenged us to find the most efficient and least frustrating route, they also required us to navigate carefully through a deadly minefield of glaciers, crevasses, and unreliable ice towers.*

Photo 3.3 *Traversing the famous ice falls of Manaslu (8163m) we faced unpredictable ice towers hanging above us which made the crossing of this section so dangerous. This is the reason why we left space between each other so that not everyone would be affected by such ice giants collapsing. In 2007 we had experienced how massive ice blocks had knocked out an entire high camp at Manaslu overnight. Fortunately, nobody had been up in that camp that particular night.*

TRADITIONAL FORMS OF UNCERTAINTY IN BUSINESS AND MANAGEMENT

Uncertainty has been defined as 'a sense of doubt that blocks or delays action',[4] implying that uncertainty is a subjective perception and is based on an individual's sense-making.[5] Traditionally, business and management disciplines have been largely based on a rational choice model of planning and decision-making that assumed that uncertainty was straightforward, and managers could achieve perfect prudence and farsightedness.[6] Over the years, however, this assumption has been challenged by numerous studies. Scholars of entrepreneurship and entrepreneurial processes that are inherently characterized by financial uncertainties and risks have introduced conceptual ideas around effectuation.[7] The latter explains how entrepreneurs base their decisions on the affordable loss principle – how much one is willing to lose – rather than on the maximization of expected returns.[8]

Within economics, Nobel Prize winner Daniel Kahneman together with Amos Tversky proposed prospect theory as a behavioral economic model, describing how people decide between alternatives that involve economic risk and uncertainty. According to these two writers people think in terms of expected utility relative to a certain reference point rather than absolute outcomes.[9] These two perspectives and numerous other economic models of uncertainty[10] have been influencing business founders and organizational decision makers. Yet, the different concepts imply that decision makers need to make the time to explore statistical probabilities,[11] subjective probabilities,[12] and various alternatives and options before making their decisions and taking actions. And, even if these decisions lead to organizational failures, the consequences for individuals will hardly ever be of a fatal nature.

UNCERTAINTIES WITH A SENSE OF URGENCY AND SEVERE CONSEQUENCES

The type of uncertainty that Ben has described is different from the aforementioned financial and economic uncertainties and their accompanying models and theories. Ben's uncertainty is characterized by a sense of urgency and by the severe consequences in the case of failing to act or in making a mistake. In the situations of uncertainty that Ben has described, effectuation principles such as the 'lemonade principle' – 'mistakes and surprises are inevitable and can be used to look for new opportunities'[13] – will most likely not work as in the case of a mistake there would just not be another opportunity. Therefore, one might argue that the uncertainties that Ben and his climbing partners are facing on their tours are not only different but seemingly incompatible with or irrelevant to those with which managers and organizations are confronted – unless the latter are mountain rescue teams or military mountain troops.

Yet, according to well-known American organizational theorist Karl Weick, the opposite is true. Organizations and their leaders face all kinds of unpredictable challenges that are of an urgent nature and that could have severe consequences for their different stakeholders.[14] Decision makers and organizations operate today in a world that is rapidly changing and that has become increasingly complex and uncertain. Like Ben, organizations and their leaders face many known unknowns or subjective dangers.[15] When in 2017 Hurricane Irma hit Florida, organizations and their members knew well beforehand about its impending arrival. However, nobody could predict with any certainty how hard and exactly where the storm would strike. And then there are the complete unknowns or objective dangers.[16] In 2008 nobody at the Oberoi Trident or the Taj Palace & Tower hotels in Mumbai could foresee or anticipate that they would be attacked by members of the Islamic terrorist organization Lashkar-e-Taiba. The consequences in both cases were of a fatal nature.

For leaders and decision makers to assume that their organizations are stable and that they know what is going to happen next is illusive, arrogant, and dangerous. Dangerous, according to Weick, in that when the unexpected does happen 'we are all the more likely to become so paralyzed that we cannot survive the experience'[17]; and illusive in believing that 'luck can be tamed by actors' wills'.[18] Nonetheless most companies and their leaders today continue to be 'hugely unprepared for the unpredictable'.[19] This comes as a surprise when considering that even 'everyday problems escalate to disaster status very quickly when people don't respond appropriately to signs of trouble'.[20]

This unpreparedness comes even more as a surprise when considering the many organizations and professions that face the types of uncertainties that are similar to those that Ben has described, and from which other organizations and decision makers could learn. Like Ben, these so-called High Reliability Organizations (HROs)[21] face uncertainties that are characterized by a sense of urgency and by the severe or fatal consequences when things go wrong. HROs include nuclear power plants, air traffic control teams, fire-fighting units, medical teams in emergency trauma centers, and military units operating in war zones – all of whom cannot afford to make mistakes. Just as Ben is constantly at high alert and continuously observes his environment for any details that indicate potential risks on his ascents and descents, so are HROs extremely attentive to potential failures and hazards and are able to scan for extremely small warning signals and changes in their organizational environments and processes.

ATTENTION TO DETAIL

The constant scanning and attentiveness require a strong focus on detail. The attention to detail does not only ensure the minimization of the particular uncertainties and risks in HROs, but it is also a key characteristic for successful company leaders of non-HROs. As Virgin Group founder Sir Richard Branson explains, 'After all, each airline uses the same planes as we all buy them from Boeing or Airbus, but you have a blank sheet of paper to work with [...] The truth is, you just need to get every single detail right'.[22] It does not come as a surprise then that CEOs such as Satya Nadella (Microsoft), Mary Barra (General Motors), and Jeff Bezos (Amazon) have all an engineering background – or, in other words, educational experiences which are known to be very detailed oriented.

CONTEXTUAL COMPLEXITY, SYSTEMIC THINKING, AND SENSE MAKING

When facing uncertainty, Weick juxtaposes the attention to detail with acknowledging and responding to contextual complexity. In his view too many executives 'underestimate the complexity of their own organizations and environments [...] leaders must complicate themselves'.[23] Systemic thinking and sense-making have been hailed as means for decision makers to addressing organizational and contextual complexities and their uncertainties more effectively.[24] Systemic thinking includes three skill sets including synthetic thinking, dynamic thinking, and closed-loop thinking. Synthetic thinking focuses on studying 'the role and purpose of a system and its parts to understand why they behave as they do'.[25] It is an important cognitive process that helps decision makers to understand the context in which a system such as an organization operates, the roles that this organization plays within a given context, and the behaviors of this organization based on such roles.[26] Dynamic and closed-loop thinking examine 'how the system and its parts behave over time' and 'how the parts of a system react and interact to each other and external factors'.[27] Within complex systems, causes and effects are often separated in both time and space, solutions often have contradictory effects in the short and long term, and subsystems engage and interrelate through multiple nonlinear causal and feedback loops.[28] Decision makers who do not understand these dynamics and characteristics of complex systems construct views of the world based on a simplified perspective,[29] and ruled by deterministic certainty by which 'action reliably leads to the same consequence'.[30]

Sense-making has been described as a process of reducing complexity and structuring ambiguous signals[31] through which people 'engage ongoing circumstances from which they extract cues and make plausible sense retrospectively, while enacting more or less order into those ongoing circumstances'.[32] By filtering through their cognitive frames, people reduce the amount and complexity of information they notice, process, and interpret along the mental templates of their cognitive frames, which then shapes the decisions and actions they take.[33] In this way, 'sense-making allows decision makers to deal with uncertainty and ambiguity by creating rational accounts of the world that enable action'.[34]

ALERTNESS AND ROUTINES

In HROs the permanent concern with warning signals, risk assessments, and failures requires all organizational members to be extremely sensitivity and attentive – as Weick's example of power plants illustrates:

> Concerns about failure are what give nuclear power plants their distinctive quality. But since complete failures in nuclear power plants are extremely rare, the people working there are preoccupied with something they seldom see. And this requires a special kind of alertness. Workers in these facilities do not monotonously watch dials, read printouts, or manipulate graphic displays and then breathe wearily at the end of the day: "Terrific – I've just had another dull, normal day." On the contrary, these workers make judgments and adjustments and comparisons to keep their days dull and normal. Of course, there is undoubtedly a kind of obsessiveness in all this, which is true of all HROs and which can make them unpleasant places to work in. But the minute a nuclear-plant worker says, "Hey, this job is boring," there is the danger that he'll stop making the fine-tuned adjustments needed to keep the job unexciting. And we all know how catastrophic it can be when things get exciting in a nuclear power plant.[35]

This alertness is not only critical to HROs but for organizations and individuals in any area of life facing uncertainties with potentially severe consequences. Regardless whether it is the nuclear power plant manager, rock climber, or free diver, when casualness and routines substitute alertness, then mistakes and accidents are preprogrammed.

That said, routines and automations are as important as alertness, and they should be juxtaposed. While alertness detects any deviation from the expected, routines and automated behaviors are vital mechanism in addressing these potential dangers and risks simultaneously to their discovery. Key to creating these routines is training, visual run-throughs, rehearsals and their analysis, revisions, and adjustments – as Weick has described in his studies of HROs at an organizational level,[36] Ben at an individual level in the previous chapter, or as American free climber icon Alex Honnold explains when describing his preparation for the free soloing of the 1000m El Capitan wall in Yosemite Park in 2017 – until then considered an unclimbable wall without a rope:

> mostly visualization was about feeling the texture of each hold in my hand and imagining the sensation of my leg reaching out and placing my foot just so. I'd imagine it all like a choreographed dance thousands of feet up. As I practiced the moves, my visualization turned to the emotional component of a potential solo. Basically, what if I got up there and it was too scary? What if I was too tired? What if I couldn't quite make the kick? I had to consider every possibility while I was safely on the ground, so that when the time came and I was actually making the moves without a rope, there was no room for doubt to creep in. Doubt is the precursor to fear, and I knew that I couldn't experience my perfect moment if I was afraid. I had to visualize and rehearse enough to remove all doubt. But beyond that, I also visualized how it would feel if it never seemed doable. What if, after so much work, I was afraid to try? What if I was wasting my time and I would never feel comfortable in such an exposed position? There were no easy answers, but El Cap meant enough to me that I would put in the work and find out.[37]

While Alex Honnold and Ben visualize and train over and over again their moves and techniques, so do surgeons, pilots, and soldiers automate their responses to every expectable and somewhat unexpected situation.

When in January 2009 Chesley B. Sullenberger was piloting US Airways flight 1549 from New York's LaGuardia airport to Charlotte he made an emergency landing on the Hudson River after geese were sucked into the jet's engines and one of the latter failed. According to traffic controllers, Sullenberger was extraordinarily calm and concentrated, 'there was no panic, no hysterics, […] It was professional, it was methodical'.[38] It was one of the unexpected events for which Sullenberger had trained for 30 years as a pilot for US Airways and the US Air Force, receiving countless training sessions in safety reliability methods, technical safety strategies, and emergency management procedures. These routines and his alertness helped him to land the plane with hardly a scratch in the middle of New York's Hudson River.

Neuroscientists have shown that mental rehearsals impact cognitive processes such as motor control and memorizing, and increase states of flow.[39] And it is these states of flow in which seemingly paradoxical mechanisms such as automated behaviors and high alertness can co-exist and synergize for individuals to be able to merge action and awareness.[40] The speed at which this merger takes place depends on pattern recognition. Within the field of cognitive neuroscience pattern recognition is defined as a cognitive process by which information about an object or event is matched with memory stored in one's limbic system of the brain.[41] In states of flow the brain releases dopamine and norepinephrine which amplify pattern recognition. Individuals can think faster and therefore they can decide faster. One moves from the conscious to a subconscious state of mind. The latter 'is far more efficient. It can process more data in much shorter time frames'[42] – enhancing further the speed of decision making. When Ben describes some of his decisions in highly uncertain situations as intuitive, he refers to this subconscious pattern-recognition intensified by neurochemicals. In such a flow state Ben is able to detect, reflect, analyze, and react simultaneously and immediately – critical in highly uncertain situations with potentially fatal consequences.

But it is not only extreme athletes like Ben or pilots like Sullenberger who can experience these flow states. Individuals with a growth mindset are well dispositioned to enter and stay in such a state. According to Stanford University psychologist Carol Dweck individuals with a growth mindset are characterized by their belief 'that their most basic abilities can be developed through dedication and hard work – brains and talent are just the starting point'. Growth minds consider personal development, learning, and self-reflection 'essential for great accomplishments'.[43]

LUCK

It is this learning and self-reflection that lead to Ben's final key observation in this chapter about uncertainty – the notion of luck. When looking back and reflecting on his reactions in high uncertainty situations, Ben recognizes that luck has played an important role in a number of his endeavors – in particular during his early, impetuous years. This stock taking is critical in the assessment or in changes of the assessment of what – if any – role luck has been playing in one's personal or professional life.[44] Alex Honnold went through a similar self-critical analysis process after his first free solo climb of Half Dome – a 600m wall in Yosemite Park:

> I'd succeeded in the solo and it was celebrated as a big first
> in climbing. But I was unsatisfied. I was disappointed in my
> performance, because I knew that I had gotten away with something.
> I didn't want to be a lucky climber. I wanted to be a great
> climber. I actually took the next year or so off from free soloing,
> because I knew that I shouldn't make a habit of relying on luck'.[45]

Based on their awareness, Ben and Alex have had the opportunity to make significant changes in their approaches to speed climbing adventures and free soloing rock walls.

While luck has rarely been at the center stage of scholarly works in the management literature there have been numerous studies highlighting 'luck as an alternative explanation for performance differences between individuals and organizations'.[46] Based on the theory of attribution[47] 'individuals tend to attribute an observed outcome to luck [instead of skill, effort and task difficulty] when the cause of the outcome is considered to be external, unstable, and uncontrollable'.[48] In contrast to Ben, however, many decision makers only 'appreciate the role of (bad) luck in failures', and only few acknowledge its role when it comes to the success and achievements on the job.

Take the example of former Renault-Nissan CEO Carlos Ghosn and his successful turn-around of Nissan in early 2000. Ghosn was celebrated as a transcultural leader by the media, business observers, and business schools alike. But the success of his initiatives enforcing the necessary organizational changes at Nissan was due to 'one large stroke of luck'.[49] At the same time as Ghosn arrived, the well-known Japanese financial house Yamaichi went bankrupt. In contrast to past practices of bailing out Japanese companies, this time the Japanese government did not intervene and help. Ghosn could now develop a strong sense of urgency amongst Nissan employees; repeating again and again that 'their fate would be no different [to Yamaichi] if they did not pull all of their efforts into figuring out, and then executing, the best way to turn Nissan around'.[50]

Often decision makers mistake luck for skill. This self-serving bias can lead 'to over-learning from successes and under-learning from failures',[51] resulting in an illusion of control[52] and overconfidence.[53] According to Weick,

> if you tried telling today's leaders to accept the fact that they're not quite as rational, deliberate, and intentional as they claim to be – and that that's okay, because that's the way humans are – I think most executives wouldn't understand. They've internalized the pressure to be perfect.[54]

This pressure has built up over time through organizations holding 'executives to standards of rationality, clarity, and foresight that are unobtainable. Most leaders can't meet such standards because they're only human, facing a huge amount of unpredictability and all the fallible analyses that we have in this world'.[55] Accepting that one cannot be perfect or perfectly prepared for every situation regardless how unexpected or unpredictable the latter might be, provides a much needed – what Ben calls – 'lightness' for decision makers facing today's increasingly complex and uncertain world. More about lightness in Chapter 9.

Following are key arguments and activities which help to understand and address uncertainties that are characterized by their sense of urgency and their severe consequences.

KEY ARGUMENTS AND TAKEAWAYS:

- Introduce mechanisms which scan for extremely small warning signals and changes in the organizational environment and organizational processes to detect potential risks, failures, and hazards very early on.
- Juxtapose the attention to detail with acknowledging and responding to contextual complexities to address their uncertainties effectively.
- Understand the context in which an organization operates, the different roles that an organization plays within a given context, and the behaviors of the organization based on such roles to respond effectively to organizational complexities, uncertainties, and dynamics.
- Understand that causes and effects are often separated in both time and space, solutions often have contradictory effects in the short and long term, and subsystems engage and interrelate through multiple nonlinear causal and feedback loops.

Understanding these dynamics helps you to construct a more complex world view and challenges deterministic certainty of actions and their outcomes.

- Juxtapose routines and automation with a sense of organizational and individual mindfulness and alertness. Mindfulness and alertness help you to detect any deviation from the expected; routines and automated behaviors help you to respond effectively to the unexpected.
- Learn equally from success and failures. Don't mistake luck for skill to prevent over-learning from successes and under-learning from failures, and to avoid a sense of overconfidence and the illusion of control.
- Accept that one cannot be perfect or perfectly prepared for every situation regardless how unexpected or unpredictable the latter might be. This provides the lightness decision makers need when facing today's increasingly complex and uncertain world.

NOTES

1 Jan Lepoutre is a professor at ESSEC Business School in France.
2 Thomas Huber in a documentary about his life on German TV BR3 at https://www.br.de/br-fernsehen/sendungen/lebenslinien/thomas-huber-huber-buam-bergsteiger-base-jumping100.html
3 See also *New York Times* article 'Free diver Natalia Molchanova descends for fun, then vanishes' at https://www.nytimes.com/2015/08/05/sports/natalia-molchanova-champion-free-diver-is-missing-near-ibiza.html
4 Lipshitz, R. and Strauss, O. 1997. Coping with uncertainty: A naturalistic decision-making analysis. *Organizational Behavior and Human Decision Processes*, 69(2), 149–163 (page 150). See also McMullen, J. and Shepherd, D. 2006. Entrepreneurial action and the role of uncertainty in the theory of the entrepreneur. *Academy of Management Review*, 31(1), 132–152.
5 Weick, K. 1979. Cognitive processes in organizations. *Research in Organizational Behavior*, 1(1), 41–74.

6 See Ansoff, H., Declerck, R. and Hayes, R. 1976. *From strategic planning to strategic management*. New York: John Wiley and Sons.

7 Saras Sarasvathy has been a key writer when it comes to entrepreneurship and effectuation. The effectuation model is discussed in detail in Dew, N., Read, S., Sarasvathy, S. and Wiltbank, R. 2008. A behavioral theory of the entrepreneurial firm. *Journal of Economic Behavior and Organization*, 66(1), 37–59 and Sarasvathy, S. 2001. Causation and effectuation: Toward a theoretical shift from economic inevitability to entrepreneurial contingency. *Academy of Management Review*, 26(2), 243–263.

8 See Sarasvathy, S. 2001. Causation and effectuation: Toward a theoretical shift from economic inevitability to entrepreneurial contingency. *Academy of Management Review*, 26(2), 243–263.

9 Kahneman, D. and Tversky, A. 1979. Prospect theory: An analysis of decision under risk. *Econometrica*, 47(2), 263–292.

10 For other models, typologies, and perspectives of uncertainty see Bredillet, C., Tywoniak, S. and Tootoonchy, M. 2018. The iron triangle and the lemonade principle: Do project managers and entrepreneurs handle uncertainty in the same way? *Euram Conference*, Iceland at https://2018.euramfullpaper.org/programme/search.asp?qs=Mahshid%20Tootoonchy; Dequech, D. 2011. Uncertainty: A typology and refinements of existing concepts. *Journal of economic issues*, 45(3), 621–640.

11 See Sanderson, J. 2012. Risk, uncertainty and governance in megaprojects: A critical discussion of alternative explanations. *International Journal of Project Management*, 30(4), 432–443.

12 See Savage, L. 1972. *The foundations of statistics*. Courier Corporation.

13 Sarasvathy, S., Kumar, K., York, J. and Bhagavatula, S. 2014. An effectual approach to international entrepreneurship: Overlaps, challenges, and provocative possibilities. *Entrepreneurship Theory and Practice*, 38(1), 71–93.

14 A conversation between Diane Coutu and Karl Weick. 2003. Sense and reliability. *Harvard Business Review*, April, 83–90 (page 85).

15 See for more details on objective and subjective dangers Csikszentmihalyi, M. 1990. *Flow: The psychology of optimal experience*. New York: HarperCollins Publishers (page 60).

16 See for more details on objective and subjective dangers Csikszentmihalyi, M. 1990. *Flow: The psychology of optimal experience*. New York: HarperCollins Publishers (page 60).

17 A conversation between Diane Coutu and Karl Weick. 2003. Sense and reliability. *Harvard Business Review*, April, 83–90.

18 Liu, C. and De Rond, M. 2016. Good night, and good luck. *The Academy of Management Annals*, DOI: 10.1080/19416520.2016.1120971.

19 A conversation between Diane Coutu and Karl Weick. 2003. Sense and reliability. *Harvard Business Review*, April, 83–90.

20 A conversation between Diane Coutu and Karl Weick. 2003. Sense and reliability. *Harvard Business Review*, April, 83–90 (page 86).

21 Weick, K. and Sutcliffe, K. 2001. *Managing the unexpected: Resilient performance in an age of uncertainty.* Hoboken, NJ: Wiley; Weick, K. and Sutcliffe, K. 2015. *Managing the unexpected: Sustained performance in a complex world.* Hoboken, NJ: Wiley

22 Sir Richard Branson at https://www.virgin.com/richard-branson/be-obsessed-details-details-details

23 A conversation between Diane Coutu and Karl Weick. 2003. Sense and reliability. *Harvard Business Review*, April, 83–90 (page 86).

24 See Polman, P. 2012. *Global Peter Drucker forum: Audio transcription of Paul Polman Panel.* http://ccdl.libraries.claremont.edu/cdm/ref/collection/twi/id/59

25 Atwater, B., Kannan, V. and Stephens, A. 2008. Cultivating systemic thinking in the next generation of business leaders. *Academy of Management Learning and Education*, 7(1), 9–25 (page 13)

26 Ackoff, R.L. (2004). *Transforming the systems movement.* Keynote Address for International Conference on Systems Thinking in Management. Philadelphia, PA. http://www.acasa.upenn.edu/RLAConfPaper.pdf

27 Atwater, B., Kannan, V. and Stephens, A. 2008. Cultivating systemic thinking in the next generation of business leaders. *Academy of Management Learning and Education*, 7(1), 9–25.

28 Forrester, J. 1971. The counterintuitive behavior of social systems. *Technology Review*, 73(3), 52–68; Richmond, B. 2000. *The thinking in systems thinking: Seven essential skills.* Waltham, MA: Pegasus Communications Inc.

29 Atwater, B., Kannan, V. and Stephens, A. 2008. Cultivating systemic thinking in the next generation of business leaders. *Academy of Management Learning and Education*, 7(1), 9–25 (page 12); Sterman, J. 2000. *Business dynamics: Systems thinking and modeling for a complex world.* Boston, MA: Irwin-McGraw-Hill.

30 Bredillet, C., Tywoniak, S. and Tootoonchy, M. 2018. The iron triangle and the lemonade principle: Do project managers and entrepreneurs handle uncertainty in the same way? *Euram Conference*, Iceland at https://2018.euramfullpaper.org/programme/search.asp?qs=Mahshid%20Tootoonchy

31 Maitlis, S., and Christianson, M. 2014. Sensemaking in organizations: Taking stock and moving forward. *Academy of Management Annals*, 8(1), 57–125; Weick, K. 1995. *Sense making in organizations*. Thousand Oaks, CA: Sage.

32 Weick, K., Sutcliffe, K. and Obstfeld, D. 2005. Organizing and the process of sensemaking. *Organization Science*, 16(4), 409–421 (page 409).

33 Daft, R. and Weick, K. 1984. Toward a model of organizations as interpretation systems. *Academy of Management Review*, 9(2), 284–295.

34 Maitlis, S. 2005. The social processes of organizational sensemaking. *Academy of Management Journal*, 48(1), 21–49 (page 21).

35 A conversation between Diane Coutu and Karl Weick. 2003. Sense and reliability. *Harvard Business Review*, April, 83–90 (page 86).

36 Weick, K. and Sutcliffe, K. 2001. *Managing the unexpected: Resilient performance in an age of uncertainty*. Hoboken, NJ: Wiley; Weick, K. and Sutcliffe, K. 2015. *Managing the unexpected: Sustained performance in a complex world*. Hoboken, NJ: Wiley.

37 Alex Honnold at TED 2018. At https://www.ted.com/talks/alex_honnold_how_i_climbed_a_3_000_foot_vertical_cliff_without_ropes/transcript?language=en#t-126361

38 CNN. 2009. Pilot praised for masterful landing, at http://edition.cnn.com/2009/TRAVEL/01/15/usairways.landing/index.html

39 Csikszentmihalyi, M. 1990. *Flow: The psychology of optimal experience*. New York: HarperCollins Publishers.

40 See Kotler, S. and Wheal, J. 2017. *Stealing fire*. New York: HarperCollins; Kotler, S. 2014. *The rise of superman*. New York: HarperCollins.

41 Nolen-Hoeksema, S., Fredrickson, B., Loftus, G. and Wagenaar, W. 2009. *Atkinson and Hilgard's introduction to psychology*. Andover, UK: Cengage Learning.

42 Kotler, S. and Wheal, J. 2017. *Stealing fire*. New York: HarperCollins; Kotler, S. 2014. *The rise of superman*. New York: HarperCollins (page 16).

43 Carol Dweck at https://mindsetonline.com/whatisit/about/index.html

44 Rescher, N. 1995. *Luck: The brilliant randomness of everyday life*. Pittsburgh, PA: University of Pittsburgh Press.

45 Alex Honnold at TED 2018. At https://www.ted.com/talks/alex_honnold_how_i_climbed_a_3_000_foot_vertical_cliff_without_ropes/transcript?language=en#t-126361

46 Liu, C. and De Rond, M. 2016. Good night, and good luck. *The Academy of Management Annals*, DOI: 10.1080/19416520.2016.1120971, (page 1).

47 For more details about Attribution Theory see Hewstone, M. 1989. *Causal attribution: From cognitive processes to collective beliefs.* London: Wiley-Blackwell; Weiner, B., Frieze, I., Kukla, A., Reed, L., Rest, S. and Rosenbaum, R.M. 1971. *Perceiving the cause of success and failure.* New York, NY: General Learning Press.

48 Liu, C. and De Rond, M. 2016. Good night, and good luck. *The Academy of Management Annals.* DOI: 10.1080/19416520.2016.1120971, (page 6).

49 Millikin, J. and Fu, D. 2003. *The global leadership of Carlos Ghosn.* Thunderbird School of Management (p. 7).

50 Millikin, J. and Fu, D. 2003. *The global leadership of Carlos Ghosn.* Thunderbird School of Management (p. 7).

51 Liu, C. and De Rond, M. 2016. Good night, and good luck. *The Academy of Management Annals.* DOI: 10.1080/19416520.2016.1120971, (page 6).

52 Langer, E. 1975. Illusion of control. *Journal of Personality and Social Psychology*, 32(2), 311–328.

53 Camerer, C. and Lovallo, D. 1999. Overconfidence and excess entry: An experimental approach. *American Economic Review*, 89(1), 306–318.

54 A conversation between Diane Coutu and Karl Weick. 2003. Sense and reliability. *Harvard Business Review*, April, 83–90 (page 89).

55 A conversation between Diane Coutu and Karl Weick. 2003. Sense and reliability. *Harvard Business Review*, April, 83–90 (page 89).

CHAPTER FOUR

About fear

SUBTEXT: Feeling the fear to appreciate life[1]

Fear has been an important aspect in my mountaineering career and in many other areas of my life – from my role as a company leader to my responsibilities as a father and husband. There are two types of fear for me. Firstly, there is the fear of an event, activity, or situation that I know about, that I expect. Just like my first ascent of an 8000m peak, the Gasherbrum 2. It was not the height of the mountain, or the uncertain weather and snow conditions, that I feared. I was really scared of the downhill skiing. I knew that the descent was extremely steep and that I had to somehow get down. That in itself already made me fill my pants. But all of this in a low oxygen environment made it even worse. So how did I try to reduce or overcome this fear?

I exposed myself to the causes of my fears. I trained deliberately and regularly the confrontation of my fears. I put myself continuously into situations with the same cause of fear, and increased slowly the fear factor levels. In other words, I trained on every steep wall in the Karwendel and many other mountain ranges. I started with a somewhat easy or not so steep wall, and moved on to more extreme walls which would come close in steepness to the one of Gasherbrum 2. I perfected and automated every move and felt eventually technically prepared for the downhill part of Gasherbrum 2.

Whenever possible I also shared or split my fears with others. In particular with my mountaineering partner Sebastian 'Basti' Haag. While he was pretty scared and worried whether he could make it to the top of Gasherbrum 2, I was fearful of not getting down in one piece on my skies. But at the same time, my strength has always been the ascending part where I could push Basti with me; and Basti had extremely strong nerves and was technically at another level when it comes to the downhill skiing – so he 'pulled' me with him. In other words, by making this first jump on the Gasherbrum 2 peak into that steep slope that was bordered by Pakistan, China and India, Basti showed me that it was possible. Without him having taken the lead in this situation I don't know if I would have had the courage to jump into this steep slope. I was able to observe where he set his turns, which route he took, and then follow his traces. But of course that takes a lot of trust in each other.

In all of this, facing and overcoming my fears motivation plays a critical role. If my motivation or will to make it to the top and back down of the mountain is not there, then I do not see the reason why I should face the fears that come with the challenge and train to overcome them. Yet at the same time, it is these fears of failure and of not making it which spark in me the motivation and will to face the challenge. Fear and motivation become codependent and reciprocal.

For me this type of fear is not only a critical aspect when it comes to what makes me thrive, but also to find out my limits and boundaries, and to know how far I can push them. Working with my fears of an extremely steep downhill ski descent, and understanding and dealing with these fears, have a great impact on my understanding of myself. Of course, it is often a dangerous balancing act of pushing the boundaries further or holding back in risky and dangerous situations. I think much comes with experiences. In retrospect, I believe that my most scary moments were situations during my early mountaineering tours, when I was not even aware of the dangers into which I put myself. In these moments of devilment and recklessness I ignored my fears and was plain lucky to have survived.

Like in 2003, my first speed trip to the Mont Blanc at 4808m. Basti and myself wanted to climb Mont Blanc in one go starting at the Mont Blanc tunnel at 1274m. At the Abri Vallot booth at 4362m a serious wind storm hit us. But we ignored the storm and the warnings of mountaineering groups which had abandoned their ascent attempts. We felt unbeatable, unstoppable. We continued on a thin ridge facing increasingly stronger and icier head winds. Communication was no longer possible. Our faces were frozen. And suddenly we realized we could not go back. Turning around would have meant that the wind would be in our backs and blowing us of the ridge. Of course, initially we were scared. But we knew we had to act if we wanted to have a chance to get out alive. And that was on what we focused. We decided to crawl on all fours up to the peak, cross it, and seek protection from the wind on the North flank of the mountain. Needless to say, I never crossed a mountain peak so quick again in my mountaineering career.

Mont Blanc taught us a valuable lesson. But this did not prevent me from getting again into other life threatening and dangerous situations. And this brings me to the other type of fear – the fear of the unknown; the fear of something unexpectedly and abruptly happening. Over the years, attentiveness and mindfulness have become crucial to me in this process of working with this type of fear. Just like in traffic or at the workplace, there are dos and don'ts on a mountain and elsewhere in nature of which one needs to be alert and mindful. This mindfulness and attentiveness are in particular critical when it comes to dealing with uncertainties. Reacting to early warning signals appropriately is not just about knowing and interpreting them correctly, but also about being attentive to them. Acting cautiously reduces my anxieties and the amount of dangerous situations. Mindfulness and attentiveness are illustrative by the calmness with which one reacts in a situation of danger. I have always been amazed by some of my mountaineering colleagues and their coolness with which they have acted in sudden situations of danger and threat. Their coolness is particular critical when they lead a group in the face of fear. I have seen many times how professional climbers' calmness has prevented their groups from panicking and led them to safety.

That does not mean that these mountaineers are not scared and have no fear. But as a mountaineer accepting those fears, and dealing correctly with them, is somewhat of a life insurance. I believe that fear is essential for survival. A mountaineer without or ignoring fear can die very quickly as he might push the limits and boundaries too far. Yet, being overly fearful and not knowing how to handle a situation of fear can also be extremely dangerous – because most likely I panic or freeze when scared. And freezing or panicking in high altitude and the freezing cold means also almost certain death. Thus, much depends on balancing fear with courage and dealing with it effectively.

Photo 4.1 *Ben skiing down the steep slopes of Broad Peak (8051m) in no fall terrain at around 6200m.*

Photo 4.2 *Ski mountaineering at its finest. Climbing buddy, friend, and working colleague Tom Steiner during a training trip in the alps.*

As Ben has highlighted in the stories above, fear has been playing a crucial role for him on and off the mountains – as a warning signal, as a self-analytical and motivational tool, and for his survival. According to social psychologists, fear and other emotions or psychological traits are the result of man's evolutionary past and serve two crucial purposes: survival and mating. In terms of survival

> fear for one's survival or fear of death from the danger or threat posed by others and the environment is absolutely essential for our survival [...] Therefore fear may be the most fundamental psychological trait that evolution has bestowed upon *Homo sapiens*.[2]

Fear has been explored by scholars in many different disciplines ranging from philosophy, physiology, psychology, medicine, biology, and neuroscience.[3] This diversity of perspectives illustrates the complexity of the concept of fear. Although fear has also been addressed by scholars in management and business disciplines, very rarely have they discussed the (neuro) physiological foundations and dynamics of fear. We believe that such an understanding of fear – even within the management or business context – is essential when exploring the behavioral consequences at an individual and organizational level.

FEAR AND THE BODILY REACTIONS AND RESPONSES

Fear is one of five core emotions. Other core emotions include happiness, sadness, anger, and shame.[4] They are 'experienced or expressed at three different, but closely interrelated levels: the mental or psychological level, the (neuro) physiological level, and the behavioral level'.[5] The emotional center responsible for these five core feelings is situated in the amygdala in the limbic system of the brain. The amygdala decodes emotions, determines possible threats, and stores fear memories. The limbic system is located between the spinal cord, through which any primary senses (everything one hears, sees, smells, tastes, or touches) enter the brain in the form of electric signals, and the rational center in which rational, logic thinking takes place.[6] Thus, all sensory information passes through the amygdala in the limbic system where emotions are produced before reaching the rational center. Any situation encountered by Ben or anybody else creates an autonomic emotional reaction which acts largely unconsciously and is out of one's control. When it comes to fear this autonomic process is crucial, as the main function of fear is to act as an early warning signal or response to acute dangers and threats.

When the amygdala associates sensory information with fear, it will project to different brain areas that mediate different fear responses depending on the context. Coping strategies can be of a passive and active nature and include the activation of stress hormones, elevated heart rate, freezing, rapid respiration, and acoustic startle.[7] American physiologist Walter Cannon described in the 1920s the acute stress response better known as the fight-or-flight response.[8] The latter is initiated by the body's release of corticoids such as cortisol and cortisone, and adrenaline and noradrenaline causing an increase in heart rate, blood pressure, breathing rate, muscle tension, and alertness. The body is preparing to either stay and face the fear causing situation, or to walk away.[9] This decision is made once the situation's electronic signals have reached the rational center and 'reason can kick into gear'.[10] Ben and anybody else need to be aware that the initial (neuro) physiological signals and responses of the mind and body are of an autonomic nature over which one cannot have control. However, what one can train and prepare for is the awareness and attentiveness to these bodily signals. But with the increasing daily attentional overloads which managers are facing, 'listening to one's body' is not a simple task or a key priority. Thus, early warning signals and responses are often either overlooked or ignored.

FEAR IN MANAGEMENT AND BUSINESS

ANXIETY OR FEAR OF THE UNKNOWN

Organizational behaviorists and management scholars have referred to some of these physiological indicators – in particular in the context of anxiety and stress management. Hans Selye extended Cannon's work and introduced a 3 Stage Stress Response Model including Cannon's alarm reaction as the first stage followed by the stages of resistance and exhaustion.[11] According to Selye, in the resistance phase the person experiencing anxiety tries to adapt to the stressor. The body releases glucocorticoids to sustain energy for dealing with the stressor and to maintain the heart rate, blood pressure, and cardiac output. In the third phase, the body runs out of energy. Constant anxiety and chronic stress are associated with high levels of circulating cortisol in the body, which can have serious implications for the immune system, digestive system, and circulatory system.[12]

Though for some commentators anxiety and fear are undistinguishable, Ben and other scholars differentiate between the two terms.[13] Similar to Ben's two types of fear, scholars consider anxiety as a 'generalized response to an unknown threat or internal conflict'[14] over which one has limited to no control. The most common causes for such anxieties or stressors amongst top managers and executives are their doubts about their reputation, about being competent enough, and feeling 'out of their usual comfort zone and on unstable grounds'[15] – also known as the 'impostor syndrome'.[16] This phenomenon was observed in therapeutic sessions with top managers. Despite their success, these executives 'had a pervasive psychological experience believing that they were intellectual frauds and feared being recognized as impostors. They suffered from anxiety, fear of failure and dissatisfaction with life'.[17] Other most common causes of anxiety and stress amongst executives are a sense of underachieving, appearing too vulnerable, being attacked or rejected by colleagues, and appearing foolish.[18]

Numerous management articles and medical studies have provided coping strategies when it comes to dealing with one's anxieties and stress, and range from relaxation techniques to biofeedback training and cognitive techniques.[19] Bestselling author Daniel Goleman,[20] who has introduced emotional and social intelligence to a broader audience, has written extensively about stress types and stress techniques such as mindfulness and (self)-awareness.[21] Besides Goleman's work, however, only few management studies and articles have considered Ben's mindfulness and attentiveness as a way to work with the fears of the uncontrollable and unexpected. Roger Jones and his study of CEOs and of what they are afraid considered awareness as the number one approach to deal with one's anxieties,[22] and Ellen Langer's extensive work on mindfulness confirms how (self)-awareness, mindfulness, and 'actively noticing [...] makes you more sensitive to context and perspective',[23] helping to identify and interpret early warning signals of potential dangers and threats ahead.

FEAR OF THE KNOWN

The term fear is considered by scholars as focusing on known external and somewhat specific dangers that are controllable and therefore manageable.[24] There are numerous studies about fear as a management tool and about the interpersonal implications of 'leading with an iron fist'.[25] These studies mostly discuss authoritative leadership styles and models proposing fear and forcefulness versus collaborative and caring forms of leading and managing.[26] Relatively little attention has been given to the fear of concrete and expected situations that Ben has described. The fear that is controllable because the situations and events are known and known to happen. When free climber Alex Honnold, was asked by American show host Jimmy Kimmel about his fears of falling off when soloing El Capitan – considered the most daring rope free climb to date – Honnold replied 'I am thinking about falling ahead of time'.[27]

Honnold prepares himself mentally and physically like Ben long before the actual situation that causes the fear. Both train the fear away step by step. Base jumper Felix Baumgartner, widely known for his stratospheric parachute jump in 2012 from almost 40km altitude, trained and prepared himself for this particular jump for around 5 years. Shortly before and during the jump fear did not cross his mind.

> You are fully focused on the jump [...] any thoughts of what could happen are completely gone [...] you have those thoughts maybe the night before or after the jump [...] during the jump you have no time for such thoughts. You are just functioning'.[28]

As well as confronting and dealing with one's fear of a situation or event long beforehand, Ben shares and splits his fears with team mates and climbing partners. Mountaineering icon Reinhold Messner explains why: 'To share the fear with somebody else leaves you with just half of the fear'.[29] This is why Messner needed more than 5 years in mental preparation for his second solo climb of an 8000m peak. During his first attempt in 1973 to solo climb the 8125m high Nanga Parpat, Messner recalls to having been scared to death of having to survive by himself: 'I was in top shape. I made it to the first third in the wall very fast. But then the fear overwhelmed me and I turned around. In that moment I would have needed a partner to share my fears'.[30] But this requires a clear understanding of what aspects of the situation cause the fear and what aspects of that fear can be controlled. An awareness of what are one's limits – physically and mentally. An understanding of how far one can shift those limits to achieve what is set out to be achieved. Fear requires the willingness for critical self-analysis, while the latter is crucial in working effectively with one's fear.[31] Fear and self-understanding become interdependent and reciprocal. Fear is an opportunity to get to know oneself and the challenge to change and grow. But as Ben mentions, much depends on one's motivation; or as sports journalist Matt Fitzgerald asks 'how bad do you want it?'.[32] This question is not only relevant for (extreme) athletes but for any professional – from managers who hesitate to take a leadership position to decision makers fearing the consequences of their decisions.

Fears of concrete situations or events exist not just in the obvious professions such as the armed forces and the fire brigade. Fears 'will always influence human beings, from the playground to the boardroom.[33]

> Workers' fear has generalized to their workplace and everything associated with work and money. We are caught in a spiral in which we are so scared of losing our jobs, or our savings, that fear overtakes our brains. And while fear is a deep-seated and adaptive evolutionary drive for self-preservation, it makes it impossible to concentrate on anything but saving our skin.[34]

Any professional in any profession comes to a point in her or his career where she or he fears to fail, fears to suffer, fears to change, and fears the consequences of her or his decisions.

Neuroeconomist Gregory Berns has shown how fear can lead to irrational decision making. In an experiment Berns and his colleagues attached electrodes to the tops of participants inside an MRI. scanner:

> The kicker was that they had to wait for the shocks. Every trial began with a statement of how big the shock would be and how long they would have to wait for it: a range of one to almost 30 seconds. For many people, the wait was worse than the shock. Given a choice, almost everyone preferred to expedite the shock rather than wait for it. Nearly a third feared waiting so much that, when given the chance, they preferred getting a bigger shock right away to waiting for a smaller shock later. It sounds illogical, but fear – whether of pain or of losing a job – does strange things to decision-making.[35]

Combining such decision-making dynamics under such conditions with the endowment effect – 'the innate tendency to value things you own more highly than everyone else does'[36] – 'we tend to hold onto what we have. When everyone does this at once, the result is a downward economic spiral'.[37]

Scholars have also shown that fear influences our judgment about the frequency of various risks. Researchers concluded that such an influence occurs 'because emotions activate tendencies to reproduce the same cognitive appraisals that initially produced the emotion'.[38] In other words, when feeling fear one appraises 'subsequent circumstances as uncertain and uncontrollable and thus causes us to see future risks as more likely'.[39] The implications of these dynamics are resistance to change and holding onto the status quo – at an individual and organizational level. In a rapidly changing and highly competitive environment this stand-still has serious consequences in terms of competitiveness and progress. Organizations fail to compete and managers are left behind in their careers.

As well as these irrational and risk-adverse decision-making dynamics, fear can create dysfunctional behaviors such as

> lack of honest conversations, too much political game playing, silo thinking, lack of ownership and follow-through, and tolerating bad behaviors, focusing on survival rather than growth, inducing bad behavior at the next level down, and failing to act unless there's a crisis.[40]

In other words, fear has not only physiological implications, but it greatly influences workers, managers, and decision makers in their daily work lives. Fear goes beyond anxiety and stress. Fear goes beyond its role as a leadership style. Fear can play an important role in developing greater self-awareness and has serious consequences in decision making processes, in the assessment of the future, and for organizational and managerial dynamics. Understanding the complexities of fear is critical not only for climbing a mountain safely but also for progressing as an organization and as individuals.

Yet, despite the consequences and implications of fear for individuals and organizations, very few managers are aware or understand their fears, and even fewer talk openly about them. Top managers often present themselves as fearless even though 'the guise of "bulletproof CEO" has systematically failed'.[41] But just as Ben and many other extreme athletes admit and talk publicly about their fears, executives might want to consider acknowledging their fears openly. Acknowledging that we have fears and 'are works in progress, allows for others to relate to us and support us. The self-awareness that may ensue from engaging openly with our vulnerabilities is a coveted leadership attribute', and a starting point to work on our fears.[42]

KEY ARGUMENTS AND TAKEAWAYS:

- Listen to your body. Be aware that physiological responses to fear are automated and cannot be controlled. Being attentive to these bodily responses will help you to recognize early warning signals and respond to acute dangers and threats.

- Understand your fears. Being able to distinguish between anxieties of the unknown und unexpected and fears of the known and expected will help you to focus on what is controllable and manageable.
- Use mindfulness and attentiveness as a way to work with the fears of the uncontrollable and unexpected. It makes you more sensitive to context and perspective and helps you to identify and interpret early warning signals of potential dangers and threats ahead.
- Split or share certain aspects of your fear with others. This reduces your fears.
- Step by step train your fears away prior to the actual situation that causes the fear. This frees energy for greater attention and focus and creates a lightness and calmness for the originally feared situation or task at hand.
- Understand that fear requires the willingness for critical self-analysis while the latter is crucial in working effectively with one's fear. Fear becomes an opportunity to get to know yourself and your limits and to face the challenge to change and grow.
- Understand that fear can lead to irrational decisions and other dysfunctional behaviors. This helps you in your decision-making process and to make better decisions.
- Be aware that fear can lead one to assess subsequent circumstances as uncertain and uncontrollable and to consider future risks as more likely. This awareness is the starting point for responding effectively to resistance to change and for engaging in progress – critical to competitiveness at an individual and organizational level.
- Deal with your fears openly. Admitting your vulnerability makes you authentic, creates relatedness and trust. And only when there is trust will employees follow. And only when employees are following will you be a leader.

NOTES

1 Quote by a mountaineering legend Hans Kammerlander in his book *Höhen und Tiefen meines Lebens*.

2 Tang, S. 2010. The social evolutionary psychology of fear and trust. At http://www.sirpalib.fudan.edu.cn/_upload/article/4d/b1/c34714544c1d94876a3d33d89953/b431562b-333b-4919-8707-e95101ea5931.pdf (page 5).

3 Steimer, T. 2002. The biology of fear and anxiety related behaviors. *Dialogues in Clinical Neuroscience*, 4(3), 231–249.

4 For more info about the different types of emotions see Julia West at http://juliahwest.com/prompts/emotion_intensity.html. For a discussion on fear and other fear-related emotions (e.g., anxiety, terror, panic) see Öhman, A. and Mineka, S. (2001). Fears, phobias, and preparedness: Toward an evolved module of fear and fear learning. *Psychological Review*, 108, 483–522.

5 Steimer, T. 2002. The biology of fear and anxiety related behaviors. *Dialogues in Clinical Neuroscience*, 4(3), page 232.

6 Bradberry and Greaves. 2009. *Emotional Intelligence 2.0*. San Diego, CA: Talent Smart.

7 Nolen-Hoeksema, S. Fredrickson, B., Loftus, G. and Wagenaar, W. 2009. *Atkinson and Hilgard's introduction to psychology*. Andover, UK: Cengage Learning.

8 Cannon, Bradford. 1994. Walter Bradford Cannon: Reflections on the man and his contributions. *International Journal of Stress Management*, 1(2).

9 Nolen-Hoeksema, S., Fredrickson, B., Loftus, G. and Wagenaar, W. 2009. *Atkinson and Hilgard's introduction to psychology*. Andover, UK: Cengage Learning.

10 Bradberry and Greaves –*Emotional Intelligence 2.0* – page 6.

11 Selye, H. 1978. *The stress of life*. New York: McGraw-Hill.

12 Selye, H. 1978. *The stress of life*. New York: McGraw-Hill.

13 Steimer, T. 2002. The biology of fear and anxiety related behaviors. *Dialogues in Clinical Neuroscience*, 4(3), 231–249.

14 Steimer, T. 2002. The biology of fear and anxiety related behaviors. *Dialogues in Clinical Neuroscience*, 4(3), page 233.

15 Lavoie, J. and Riese, J. 2018. Leaders: Its's OK to not know everything. McKinsey & Company. At https://www.mckinsey.com/business-functions/organization/our-insights/the-organization-blog/

leaders-its-ok-to-not-know-everything?cid=other-eml-alt-mip-mck-oth-1807&hlkid=d23aad80a21043cab58256df955090f4&hctky=2837206&hdpid=063cce5d-85e3-48d9-bf68-935a2be7674b

16 Jones, R. 2015. What CEOs are afraid of. *Harvard Business Review*, February. At https://hbr.org/2015/02/what-ceos-are-afraid-of

17 Sakulku, J. 2011. The Impostor Phenomenon. *The Journal of Behavioral Science*, 6(1), 75–97.

18 Jones, R. 2015. What CEOs are afraid of. *Harvard Business Review*, February. At https://hbr.org/2015/02/what-ceos-are-afraid-of ; Brandy, D. 2018. Five common fears business leaders have, and how to overcome them. *Business Insider*. At https://www.businessinsider.com.au/fear-anxiety-business-leader-2018-6

19 Goudreau, J. 2013. 12 Ways to eliminate stress at work. *Forbes*. At https://www.forbes.com/sites/jennagoudreau/2013/03/20/12-ways-to-eliminate-stress-at-work/#2297dbb57f29; Varvogli, L. and Darviri, C. 2011. Stress management techniques: evidence-based procedures that reduce stress and promote health. *Health Science Journal*. At http://www.hsj.gr/medicine/stress-management-techniques-evidencebased-procedures-that-reduce-stress-and-promote-health.php?aid=3429; Valcour, M. 2016. Managing yourself: Beating burnout. *Harvard Business Review*, November, 98–101.

20 For more information about Daniel Goleman's publications visit http://www.danielgoleman.info/purchase/

21 Goleman, D. and the Dalai Lama. 2003. *Healing emotions*. Boston, MA: Shambhala.

22 See Jones, R. 2015. What CEOs are afraid of. *Harvard Business Review*, February. At https://hbr.org/2015/02/what-ceos-are-afraid-of

23 Langer, H. 2014. Mindfulness in the age of complexity. *Harvard Business Review*, March, 68–73.

24 Steimer, T. 2002. The biology of fear and anxiety related behaviors. *Dialogues in Clinical Neuroscience*, 4(3), page 233.

25 Dib, F. 2014. Fear rots the brain. *Professional Manager*, Autumn, page 43.

26 See See Dib, F. 2014. Fear rots the brain. *Professional Manager*, Autumn, 42–45; Maccoby, M., Hoffer Gittel, J. and Ledeen, M. 2004. Leadership and the fear factor. *MIT Sloan Management Review*, Winter. At https://sloanreview.mit.edu/article/leadership-and-the-fear-factor/

27 Alex Honnold in an interview with Jimmy Kimmel. At https://www.youtube.com/watch?v=-vOcJtlTQAY

28 Televised interview with Markus Lanz on October 17, 2013. At https://www.youtube.com/watch?v=pTSzw4xac14

29 Televised interview with Markus Lanz on October 17, 2013. At https://www.youtube.com/watch?v=pTSzw4xac14

30 Televised interview with Markus Lanz on October 17, 2013. At https://www.youtube.com/watch?v=pTSzw4xac14

31 Jones, R. 2015. What CEOs are afraid of. *Harvard Business Review*, February. At https://hbr.org/2015/02/what-ceos-are-afraid-of

32 From Matt Fitzgerald's book about the psychology mind over muscle; Fitzgerald, M. 2015. *How bad do you want it?* Boulder, CO: Velo Press.

33 Jones, R. 2015. What CEOs are afraid of. *Harvard Business Review*, February. At https://hbr.org/2015/02/what-ceos-are-afraid-of

34 Berns, G. 2008. In hard times fear can impair decision making. *New York Times*. At https://www.nytimes.com/2008/12/07/jobs/07pre.html

35 Berns, G. 2008. In hard times fear can impair decision making. *New York Times*. At https://www.nytimcs.com/2008/12/07/jobs/07prc.html

36 Berns, G. 2008. In hard times fear can impair decision making. *New York Times*. At https://www.nytimes.com/2008/12/07/jobs/07pre.html

37 Berns, G. 2008. In hard times fear can impair decision making. *New York Times*. At https://www.nytimes.com/2008/12/07/jobs/07pre.html

38 Nolen-Hoeksema, S., Fredrickson, B., Loftus, G. and Wagenaar, W. 2009. *Atkinson and Hilgard's introduction to psychology*. Andover, UK: Cengage Learning, page 404.

39 Nolen-Hoeksema, S., Fredrickson, B., Loftus, G. and Wagenaar, W. 2009. *Atkinson and Hilgard's introduction to psychology*. Andover, UK: Cengage Learning, page 404.

40 Jones, R. 2015. What CEOs are afraid of. *Harvard Business Review*, February. At https://hbr.org/2015/02/what-ceos-are-afraid-of

41 Heyden, M. and Hayward, M. 2018. Why CEOs need to embrace fear. *The Conversation*. At https://theconversation.com/why-ceos-need-to-embrace-fear-96851

42 Heyden, M. and Hayward, M. 2018. Why CEOs need to embrace fear. *The Conversation*. At https://theconversation.com/why-ceos-need-to-embrace-fear-96851

CHAPTER FIVE

About failure

SUBTEXT: Failing to succeed

In my younger mountaineering years I felt really bad about failure. It was somewhat inacceptable to me. It was not an option. But this attitude or mindset changed very quickly when I started to climb my first larger mountains such as the ones in the Peruvian Andes in 2004. Peru was one of the first and biggest failures in my mountaineering career. It was a complete disaster. I, my climbing partner Basti, and another friend failed in every aspect – not only in terms of the actual mountaineering but also with regard to the preparation process and the equipment. We had no prior high-altitude mountaineering experience when we arrived in Lima. Instead we came with lots of devilment and ignorance. While today I understand that to be fast at high altitude you need to go slow, in Peru we just wanted action, action, action. We wanted to prove that we are the real cracks. And we almost killed ourselves.

Basti was sick for three days in Lima and we wanted to make up for these lost days when we arrived in Huarez, a small city at 3000m in the Peruvian Cordillera Blanca. We immediately started jogging and training. We ignored every advice to take it easy and to first acclimatize. We also ignored the many warning signals from our bodies. We were extremely badly equipped, had hardly any food, and very little water. We drank water from a river in which we found a dead cow later on higher up on the mountain. On the first day I ran up the Urus at 5495m with half a liter of water and wondered afterwards why I felt completely shattered. I used my ski mountaineering racing boots which were light but also too small. At night I had started to have nightmares and just wanted to die. My resting pulse was at 120bpm. The three of us were cramped in a two person tent. Our gasoline bottles were wrongly filled with diesel. Basti started to have pulmonary edema because we went up too fast and without acclimatization. We did everything wrong and our Peru experience was one big fiasco made up from countless smaller failures and mistakes.

In retrospect I must admit that to have such a big failure early on probably saved my life more than once on subsequent tours and expeditions. Without all these small failures and experiences in Peru I could not have been as prepared and ready as I was for my future high-altitude climbing adventures. We all agreed that in Peru we behaved really stupidly and that our Peru disaster was our own fault. We realized that any similar mistakes at even higher altitude would be fatal. We revised and corrected every aspect of our Peru trip. The Peru failure became an important learning experience. But our reflections also confirmed to us that our speed mountaineering style – ascending from Basecamp to the mountain peak and descending back down to Basecamp in one go – to be applied in high altitude made a lot of sense to us. Sleeping in different camps at high altitude on the way to the peak still gives me a headache just thinking of it. And carrying all the gear and material camp by camp upwards is not only physically extremely debilitating but it was also the riskier option for us because we wanted to spend as little time as possible in the death zone. The death zone starting at around 7000–7500m is not called this for no reason. However, everybody has to find his own climbing style and there is no right or wrong.

A year later we went for a speed ascent of Mustagh Ata (7546m) in Western China. We were extremely well prepared with months of training and the right equipment. We were acclimatized at peak fitness. We followed strictly our 'go slow to go fast' mantra for our ascents and made sure that nobody got sick. We adapted our ski mountaineering racing style and made it directly from Basecamp (4400m) to the peak in in 9 hours and 25 min, and then skied back to Basecamp in 1 hour. This had not been tried before, and we set a benchmark. But we were still hungry for more and wanted to go for our first 8000m mountain. In the summer of 2006 we climbed the Gasherbrum 2 (8035m) twice – first in the normal style with a chain of camps on the way to the peak, and five days later we speed climbed Gasherbrum 2 from advanced Basecamp (5900m) in 12.5h.

Our success at Gasherbrum 2 confirmed to us our lessons learnt and the revisions and changes we made in our mountaineering approach. Yet, despite the same professional attitude and preparation, our Manaslu (8163m) attempt a year later failed. And it was a failure of two kinds. The first type of failure was due to externalities. The weather was terrible. On one of our attempts to make it to the peak we faced winds of 100km/h and continuously fresh loads of snow which made it impossible to make it to the top. On our last attempt, 150m below the peak's ridge we were confronted with a fresh wind compressed snow field that was too dangerous to cross. Any attempt would have caused an avalanche. The other failure was my inability to accept our failure to make it to the top due to the weather. This feeling of not being in control of my own destiny was somewhat new to me, and initially I could not get to terms with this powerlessness. We left Nepal unfulfilled and frustrated, promising ourselves that we would not return for at least the next 10 years. Over the following months, however, I learnt to acknowledge that however well prepared you might be, there are externalities which can make your adventure fail and for which you cannot control. In this sense Manaslu was an as important lesson as Peru. Today, when I have an 8000m ascent or any other major project, my attitude is completely different. I accept that it is not just up to me to succeed. There is always the option that I might fail for reasons that are beyond my control. I have learnt to be patient; to ask myself how badly do I want to succeed and at what costs; and am I prepared to stand up again and again? A role model for me with regard to perseverance and determination has always been Gerlinde Kaltenbrunner, the first woman who climbed all 14 8000m peaks without oxygen. Gerlinde attempted the K2 (8611m) six times. On the sixth attempt in 2010 her friend Fredrik Ericsson died in front of her eyes on an ice slope. In 2011 she stood back up again for the seventh time to finally make it to the K2 peak.

So we also went back to our destiny mountain in 2012 – not 10 years later as planned – yet still a long 5 years of dealing with doubts and reflections. And we initially failed again to reach our goal of making it to the peak. An avalanche next to us made us abandon our ascent and help any surviving climbers. There were 11 mountaineers who did not make it. Back in Basecamp everybody was talking about the accident. The avalanche hung like a big dark cloud over the Basecamp. There was a lot negative energy and tensions. Climbers abandoned their expeditions and left the camp. Many of these climbers felt that so shortly after the accident it was not right to climb Manaslu. But then when? How long should one wait? Weeks, months, years?

Very consciously I decided to shift this experience aside, leave the avalanche behind me, and focus on climbing Manaslu. I knew I wanted to get to that peak. Yet my overall goal had changed since the avalanche. It was no longer just about making it to the top, but to make it back down in one piece. This change of goal turned the apparent failure of not having made it to the peak into a feeling of relief to be still alive and to see my kids again. I surrounded myself with people with a positive, likeminded attitude. People like Ivan Vallejo, an Ecuadorian mountaineer who climbed all 14 8000m peaks without oxygen. He really motivated and pushed me to try it again. It was like a therapy. He recharged my batteries with his positive energy. He was forward looking and confirmed to me that there was nothing wrong to retry Manaslu so shortly after the avalanche. And seven days after the accident and 15 hours of climbing I reached the Manaslu directly from Basecamp.

While we failed in Nepal in 2007 due to externalities such as cold winds and snow, and in Peru due to our individual incapability and stupidity, we failed on Broad Peak (8051m) in 2009 as a team. Mountaineering teams can face extreme pressures. Very often we spend day and night for weeks together in camps – often cramped against each other in small tents in extreme weather conditions. Communication at high altitude – where every breath is a major effort – is often reduced to a minimum. 'What if' situations and contingency plans, and individual expectations need to be discussed and agreed before an ascent – in particular when it is a speed climbing ascent. Therefore, miscommunications and different expectations can easily lead to interpersonal conflicts, which can be disastrous for mountaineering expeditions in teams. This happened to Basti and me. Despite many years of successfully working as a mountaineering team there were tensions and disagreements between us from the beginning. During our speed climbing ascent of Broad Peak we ended up turning around 20 altitude meters below the peak; and we needed 39 hours instead of the forecasted maximum 24 hours for the failed attempt. But as our joint ascent on Manaslu in 2012 showed, we learnt our lessons from this failure. While initially after Broad Peak each of us went his own way, we got together eventually and analyzed the Broad Peak expedition with a particular focus on our interpersonal conflicts. Failures are worth nothing if you do not have the ability and willingness to self-reflect and learn from your own mistakes, especially when it comes to conflicts within a team. This self-reflection and ability to analyze oneself from an outside perspective, and then take corrective and courageous actions, is crucial to remain effective and successful as a team.

I consider most of my failures not only as learning experiences and as opportunities for self-development, but also as means for greater creativity. My expeditions in Peru, Pakistan, China, and Nepal helped me to identify new ways and approaches that could make my speed climbing projects in high altitude a success. Much of my creative and innovative thinking focused on my equipment and on my preparation. On the mountain creative thinking helped me to stay calm, relaxed, and focused when facing challenging situations and potential failures. And more than once this saved my life.

Photo 5.1 *Basti Haag in a respectful gesture towards Manaslu summit (8163m) on our camp spot at 6400m. This hidden camp spot away from the big face fire line saved our lives only a couple of days later when a massive avalanche killed 11 people in the big face Basti looks into.*

COMMON RESPONSES TO FAILURES IN ORGANIZATIONS

Ben and many other extreme athletes seem comfortable and at ease when describing and discussing situations of failure – even in public. They acknowledge the importance of their failures for their personal and professional self-development and growth, and for any subsequent performances. Within an organizational and managerial context, however, most companies are 'profoundly biased against failure […] Executives hide mistakes or pretend they were always part of the master plan'.[1] Failure is often seen as a blaming opportunity rather than one of learning and change. According to well-known organizational theorist Karl Weick, it is 'idiotic' that organizations 'isolate failure, to blame the culprit, and to not learn from mistakes'.[2] Many managers fear failures because they have 'internalized the pressure to be perfect'.[3] And when managers fail they often show dysfunctional reactions that could make the situation even worse[4]: from 'panicking and throwing out the game plan' to 'scrambling for self-protection and abandoning the rest of the group. Hiding the facts and hoping that things will get better by themselves before anyone notices. Denying that there is anything to learn or change. Using decline as an excuse to let facilities or investments deteriorate'.[5]

In the USA, scholars studied several hundred thousand managers from every industry sector and identified 11 personality types whose responses to failure could derail a career. There is for example the 'Bold type, who thinks in grandiose terms, is frequently in error but never in doubt, and refuses to acknowledge his mistakes, which then snowball'; or the Mischievous type who 'denies his role in failure [and who] may deny that failure has even occurred'.[6] The scholars based their study on the works of American psychologist Saul Rosenzweig in the 1930s and 1940s.[7] Rosenzweig categorized individuals and their responses to frustrating situations such as failures into extrapunitive, impunitive, and intropunitive. Extrapunitive individuals tend to unfairly blame others – a reaction 'all too common in the business world'; impunitive individuals' either deny that failure has occurred or deny their own role in it'; and intropunitive individuals evaluate themselves too severely and consider failures where none exists.[8]

DEFINING SUCCESS TO ACKNOWLEDGING FAILURE

The different types and categories of reactions to failure illustrate that if managers want to learn and benefit from their failures like Ben and other extreme athletes, they have to first identify and acknowledge their failures. This requires clear benchmarks as to what managers consider important to them and how they define success. This can be challenging because many managers and decision makers are driven by values and definitions of success espoused by their organizations instead of being guided by their own ones.[9] In today's rapidly changing and complex environment 'nobody seems to have a real sense of who they really are any more'[10] and what is truly important to them. Managers who have established clear personal values and benchmarks of success need to regularly revise and adjust them. Ben's account of his Manaslu ascents in 2012 illustrates how different experiences and contexts can change (or can be changed by) one's perspective about what matters and what is considered a failure or success. Arianna Huffington, who founded one of the biggest media companies after her second book was rejected by 36 publishers, recalls that

> my mother used to call failure a stepping-stone to success, as opposed to the opposite of success. When you frame failure that way, it changes dramatically what you're willing to do, how you're willing to invent, and the risks you'll take.[11]

ANALYZING FAILURES

Even when managers acknowledge their failures, turning the latter into learning experiences can be a long and bumpy road. Firstly, managers have to analyze the reasons for a situation of failure 'beyond the obvious and superficial explanations'.[12] Arguments such as 'procedures were not followed' or 'the market just wasn't ready for our great new product' are shallow and do not help managers to get to the heart of the failure and understand its causes.[13] An analysis of a failure to be constructive requires a deep-digging approach and critical self-analysis. When Ben and his climbing partners came back from Peru they blamed themselves and not each other, and admitted their own recklessness, ignorance, and carelessness that led to their failure. When former Procter&Gamble (P&G) CEO A.G. Lafley wanted to better understand the effectiveness of his company's acquisition strategy he put a team at P&G together to

> do a detailed analysis of all our acquisitions from 1970 to 2000. And the sobering story was that only 25% to 30% succeeded in that period. We studied the failures in detail. We pinpointed the problems and discovered patterns in our mistakes. We found five fundamental root causes of failure.[14]

Taking responsibility for personal failures or organizational wrongdoings remains unusual amongst company leaders, decision makers, and managers alike. Shortly after the Deepwater Horizon oil spill disaster in 2010, BP's then CEO Tony Hayward explained that 'it was not our people, our systems or our processes' and instead pointed the finger at drilling company Transocean Ltd as the main culprit.[15] Seven years after the collapse of global financial services firm Lehman Brothers, its then CEO Richard Fuld continues to disavow any blame for having triggered the financial crisis, and accuses the US government of having ordered the investment bank's closure.[16] Research shows that people 'regard themselves in more favorable terms than they regard others'.[17] Past successes can make managers overconfident in their capabilities and competencies and make them deny any responsibility, or shift blame unfairly to others when confronted with failures.[18]

Such blaming patterns amongst decision makers and leaders come as a surprise when considering that very few causes of failures are causes for blame. Causes of failures that are blameworthy include deliberate or undeliberate mistakes in 'routine or predictable operations, which can be prevented'. Executives have estimated that there are only between 2–5 percent of failures in their organizations that are truly blameworthy. Causes of failures that are not blameworthy include mistakes in 'complex operations, which can't be avoided but managed so that they don't mushroom into catastrophes'; and causes of failures that could be considered as praiseworthy are 'unwanted outcomes in, for example, research settings, which are valuable because they generate knowledge.'[19] Yet, although failures that are not blameworthy or that are instead praiseworthy represent the vast majority of failures in organizations, executives admit to treating 70–90 percent of all failures as blameworthy.[20] These blaming patterns call for business leaders and managers to be more critical in their analysis of situations of failure, and in particular of their own roles and responsibilities in such situations. Jeff Bezos, founder and CEO of Amazon, admits to 'have made billions of dollars of failures at Amazon.com'.[21] But admitting one's responsibility in failures can be emotionally draining, and can take courage and time.

BOUNCING BACK AFTER FAILURE

L eaders need not only the courage to face their own imperfections and take responsibility for failures, but they also need the strength and confidence to bounce back after a failure.[22] Two individuals have been in the headlines for different reasons – but they have in common to be known for their strong wills to bounce back. Niki Lauda, a three times Formula One racing car champion and aviation entrepreneur crashed his racing car in 1976 at the Nürburgring race circuit. Despite severe burns to his scalp, forehead, ears, and hands, he was back racing six weeks later at the Monza race track, where he would be seen in the pits peeling blood-soaked bandages of his head.[23] Between 2006 and 2008, entrepreneur Elon Musk faced numerous failures at Tesla in form of crash-related battery fires and at SpaceX with rocket launch explosions – bringing both companies to the brink of bankruptcy.[24]

The list of other company founders, leaders, and decision makers who have failed dramatically and bounced back is long, and ranges from Walt Disney to Jeff Bezos, Steven Spielberg, Steve Jobs, J.K. Rowling, and

Oprah Winfrey. And as Ben has highlighted in his account earlier, Disney pointed out that 'it's important to have a good hard failure when you're young because it makes you kind of aware of what can happen to you'.[25] And just like Ben took the opportunity to learn from his Peru and Broad Peak experiences, some decision makers and company leaders bounce back by learning from their own mistakes and company failures. In the case of Elon Musk and SpaceX, for example, Musk and his engineers considered the early rocket launch and landing failures critical data collection processes for their Falcon 9 to become the first orbital class rocket capable of reflight.[26]

Yet, such examples of decision makers and their learning experiences from failures remain the exception. 'The topic of failure gets more lip service than good practice'.[27] Acknowledging failures and taking responsibility for them are important first steps; but within an organizational context such behaviors need to be institutionalized and a culture of courage, confidence, and openness needs to be created that 'turns failures into learning and leads to continual improvement'.[28] Such organizational cultural change and its outcomes are interdependent. Learning and improving enhance confidence and the courage for trying out despite potential set-backs and failures; while exploring and experimenting are prerequisites of learning and development. An illustration of this interdependency is the anecdote about the German scientist Wernher von Braun. He sent a bottle of champagne to one of his engineers 'who confessed that he might have inadvertently short-circuited the missile. An investigation revealed that the engineer was right, which meant that expensive redesigns could be avoided'.[29]

ORGANIZATIONAL CHANGES

Though champagne might be an interesting alternative incentive to change an organizational culture, many organizations have already in place methods and processes which allow for failures and encourage learning from them. And yet, although management techniques and concepts such as color-coded reports (green for good, yellow for caution, red for problems), total quality management, six sigma, and customer feedback are common practice, executives rate their organizations at a two to three (on a scale of one to 10) when it comes to effectively learning from failures.[30] For organizations to become more effective in their learning from failures, their leaders need to focus on intelligent failures.[31] These are failures which are praiseworthy and provide valuable takeaways. They have been described as outcomes of well thought through activities. They occur early on in the process, and are therefore relatively inexpensive and of a more modest scale.[32] Organizational learning from such failures starts by sharing the lessons learnt across the organization. They have to be communicated to and memorized by all employees so that the same mistakes won't happen again. Regular retrospective meetings and systematic after action reviews ingrained within the organization's culture support such organizational communication processes and dialogues.

Ben's emphasis on surrounding himself with supportive, positive, and forward thinking climbing partners and mentors in bouncing back from failures through learning and doing things differently is equally important in the business context. Of course, when teams and individuals experience failures it is important to give them some time to feel disappointed; but leaders should not let them 'get stuck in a negative, analytical mood for too long' and instead shift the focus on the future and 'more on solutions rather than problems'.[33] Organizations coming back from failures stress collaboration, common goals, and a joint vision amongst their organizational members. 'When somebody drops the ball, someone else is there to pick it up'.[34] Organizations emphasizing collaboration, accountability, and initiative strengthen employees' self-confidence and confidence in each other.[35]

Organizations which explicitly allow for failures as a learning tool provide the basis for innovation and development. According to former Facebook CIO Tim Campos:

> to be the best we need to innovate. And for people to innovate, they need the freedom to make mistakes. When you're willing to tolerate

failure, people are willing to do things differently. And if you are not willing to do things differently, you have to do it in a tried-and-true way, which is not innovative.[36]

Many companies have chosen the second option. While they espouse the virtues of innovation and creativity, their leaders 'live in fear of mistakes, missteps, and disappointments – which is why they have so little innovation and creativity'.[37]

For organizations that hand out licenses to fail to their employees, leaders and decision makers might simultaneously want to indicate the no fail zones – where failures can occur and where not. While a risk embracing and fiercely experimental company like Amazon[38] was able to compensate a big loss for having to give away for free 50 million toys due to overestimated sales forecasts,[39] such mistakes would mean the end for many other companies. Or as Ben explained, the many mistakes he made in Peru were critical but not life threatening at the time, but making one of them at 8000m would have cost his life.

Ben continues to accept that in the highly unpredictable context in which he is active, failures occur however well he is prepared. It is time for more organizations to also understand that failures are inevitable in the uncertain and rapidly changing environments in which they operate. And that what counts to sustain their business is what lessons they get out of these failures.

KEY ARGUMENTS AND TAKEAWAYS:

- Be clear about how you define success to recognize a failure.
- Report and deal with failures blame-free. Very few causes of failures are causes for blame. Most failures are intelligent failures and learning opportunities, and not blameworthy. Blame-free appraising creates a productive work environment with a focus on solutions rather than problems.

(Continued)

- Accept your failures and take responsibility for them. Nobody is perfect. Being honest about your mistakes makes you human and authentic. This can turn into respect and trust from your employees.
- Institutionalize this courage of openness and honesty within the company. It creates the basis for a company-wide engagement in learning from failures and leads to continual improvement and development of your employees and the organization as a whole.
- Critically analyze failures. By getting to the root causes of your failures you develop more learning opportunities and a wider range of solutions then by looking for the obvious and apparent explanations.
- Use your lessons learnt to bounce back. They give you courage and self-confidence and prevent you from falling back into the same track or making the same mistakes again and again.
- Share the lessons learnt across the organization and memorize them so that the same mistakes won't happen again.
- Surround yourself with collaborative and forward-thinking individuals. They strengthen your confidence and will support you to bounce back from failure.
- Accept that creativity and innovation go hand in hand with failure. Going down new paths implies to take risk and the ability to fail fast.
- When you hand out a license to fail explain the no fail zones. Certain zones mean the certain ending for certain companies.

NOTES

1 McGrath, R. 2011. Failure by design. *Harvard Business Review*, April, page 77.
2 A conversation between Diane Coutu and Karl Weick. 2003. Sense and reliability. *Harvard Business Review*, April, 83–90 (page 87).
3 A conversation between Diane Coutu and Karl Weick. 2003. Sense and reliability. *Harvard Business Review*, April, 83–90 (page 89).

4 Dattner, B. and Hogan, R. 2011. Can you handle failure? *Harvard Business Review*, April, 117–121.

5 Moss Kanter, R. 2011. Cultivate a culture of confidence. *Harvard Business Review*, April, 34.

6 Dattner, B. and Hogan, R. 2011. Can you handle failure? *Harvard Business Review*, April, 118.

7 See for example Rosenzweig, S. 1945. The picture association method and its application in a study of reactions to frustration. *Journal of Personality*, 14(2), 3–23.

8 Dattner, B. and Hogan, R. 2011. Can you handle failure? *Harvard Business Review*, April, p. 118.

9 Drucker, P. 2005. Managing oneself. *Harvard Business Review*, January, 100–109.

10 A conversation between Diane Coutu and Karl Weick. 2003. Sense and reliability. *Harvard Business Review*, April, 83–90 (page 88).

11 press farm. 2018. Nine founders who bounced back from failure to build successful companies. At https://press.farm/ founders-bounced-back-failure-build-successful-companies/

12 Edmondson, A. 2011. Strategies for learning from failure. *Harvard Business Review*, April, page 54.

13 Edmondson, A. 2011. Strategies for learning from failure. *Harvard Business Review*, April, 49–58.

14 Interview between Karen Dillon and A.G. Lafley. 2011. I think of my failures as a gift. *Harvard Business Review*, April, page 89.

15 Daily, M. 2010. BP, other oil drill companies start the blame game. *Reuters*. May 7. At https://www.reuters.com/article/us-oil-rig-blame-idUSTRE645 78H20100506

16 Braithwaite, T. 2015. Unrepentant Dick Fuld blames Washington for Lehman collapse. *Financial Times*, May 28. At https://www.ft.com/content/ a6512800-055d-11e5-8612-00144feabdc0

17 Brown, J. and McGallagher, F. 1992. Coming to terms with failure: Private self-enhancement and public self-effacement. *Journal of Experimental Social Psychology*, 28(1), 3–22 (page 3).

18 Gino, F. and Pisano, G. 2011. Why leaders don't learn from success. *Harvard Business Review*, April, 68–74.

19 These praiseworthy failures are also considered 'intelligent failures'. This term was introduced by Sim Sitkin in Sitkin, S. 1992. Learning through failure: The strategy of small losses. *Research in Organizational Behavior*, 14(2), 231–266.

20 Edmondson, A. 2011. Strategies for learning from failure. *Harvard Business Review*, April, pages 50 and 51.

21 press farm. 2018. Nine founders who bounced back from failure to build successful companies. At https://press.farm/founders-bounced-back-failure-build-successful-companies/

22 Moss Kanter, R. 2011. Cultivate a culture of confidence. *Harvard Business Review*, April, 34.

23 Radeska, T. 2017. Niki Lauda returned to racing only six weeks after his nearly fatal crash in the 1976 German Grand Prix. *The Vintage News*. At https://www.thevintagenews.com/2017/11/20/niki-lauda-returned-to-racing-only-six-weeks-after-his-nearly-fatal-crash-in-the-1976-german-grand-prix/

24 Sally, F. 2017. The many failures of Elon Musk, captured in one giant infographic. *Market Watch*. At https://www.marketwatch.com/story/the-many-failures-of-elon-musk-captured-in-one-giant-infographic-2017-05-24

25 Oh my Disney. 2018. At https://ohmy.disney.com/insider/2012/07/03/the-wonderful-world-of-walt-icon-of-the-american-experience/

26 Vance, A. 2015. *Iron man: Elon Musk's quest to forge a fantastic future*. New York: Ecco Press.

27 Interview between Karen Dillon and A.G. Lafley. 2011. I think of my failures as a gift. *Harvard Business Review*, April, page 89.

28 Interview between Karen Dillon and A.G. Lafley. 2011. I think of my failures as a gift. *Harvard Business Review*, April, page 89.

29 A conversation between Diane Coutu and Karl Weick. 2003. Sense and reliability. *Harvard Business Review*, April, 83–90 (page 87).

30 McGrath, R. 2011. Failure by design. *Harvard Business Review*, April, 77–83.

31 See Sitkin, S. 1992. Learning through failure: The strategy of small losses. *Research in Organizational Behavior*, 14(2), 231–266.

32 Sitkin, S. 1992. Learning through failure: The strategy of small losses. *Research in Organizational Behavior*, 14(2), 231–266; McGrath, R. 2011. Failure by design. *Harvard Business Review*, April, 77–83.

33 Gallo, A. 2015. How to help your team to bounce back from failure. *Harvard Business Review*, February. At https://hbr.org/2015/02/how-to-help-your-team-bounce-back-from-failure

34 Moss Kanter, R. 2011. Cultivate a culture of confidence. *Harvard Business Review*, April, 34.

35 Moss Kanter, R. 2011. Cultivate a culture of confidence. *Harvard Business Review*, April, 34.

36 Burnham, K. 2011. *Facebook's CIO shares IT innovation successes and failures.* At https://www.cio.com/article/2407573/consumer-technology/facebook-s-cio-shares-it-innovation-successes-and-failures.html

37 Taylor, B. 2017. How Coca Cola, Netflix and Amazon learn from failure. *Harvard Business Review*, November, page 3.

38 Streitfeld, D. 2017. Behind Amazon's success is an extreme tolerance for failure. *New York Times*. At https://www.seattletimes.com/nation-world/behind-amazons-success-is-an-extreme-tolerance-for-failure/

39 press farm. 2018. Nine founders who bounced back from failure to build successful companies. At https://press.farm/founders-bounced-back-failure-build-successful-companies/

CHAPTER SIX

About death and mortality

SUBTEXT: It is not those who are gone who suffer most, but those who stay

I never thought as a boy or as a teenager about death. I always believed that I will live forever. I enjoyed life and living fully the moment. And even during my first adventure trips and expeditions, death or mortality never really crossed my mind. For me, death or dead people were things you watch on television, but not something that would ever cross my path. This belief changed over time. In 2004, climbing Mustagh Ata (7546m) with my climbing partner Basti on an exploratory ascent, shortly after having passed an empty Camp 3, we walked into a frozen body covered to the hips in snow. When approaching the body, our worst fears came true. She – it was a woman – was already dead. We were too late. We knew that two members of a German expedition had been missing for two days. They were last seen trying to reach the summit. But due to dense fog (whiteout) they couldn't be seen anymore. When finding the dead woman climber, I did not spend any time thinking about death or mortality. I was just functioning. We focused on finding her climbing partner. After having searched the surrounding area unsuccessfully we decided to continue our ascent. We wanted to get a better view of the area from high above. It was freezing cold and the physical efforts to continue our ascent kept us from drifting off in our thoughts. Two hours later we stood on the Mustagh Ata summit. But real joy or happiness did not come up. Looking down onto the huge snow field below us, we could see a small black dot at the very right, next to a steeply falling ridge 200 altitude meters below the summit. That little dot did not fit into the picture of nothing but whiteness. We skied down and found the missing second member of the German expedition team. At minus 30 degrees, the climber had opened his down jacket and taken off his gloves – a reaction of people who are just about to freeze to death when they suddenly feel a sense of hot flush. While seemingly frozen, he still had an air of life in his body and we decided to bring him down to Camp 3. There another expedition which had moved up by then took care of him. It was almost dark and we were exhausted from a very long day in the freezing cold and the unexpected rescue operation. But we didn't want to spend another night at high altitude and skied further down to Basecamp. There the next morning we were informed that the man had passed away.

Of course, the death of these two German climbers touched us tremendously. It was a brutal and somewhat scary wake-up call or hint of our own mortality, and we discussed whether or not we still wanted to try our speed climbing attempt the next day. But it was never a real question. Of course we wanted; this was what we had come for. Thus, a few days later, we speed climbed Mustagh Ata from Basecamp in less than 10 hours. When we passed the dead woman again, I was no longer scared. It has become the bitter reality for me that some of us stay on the mountains while others make it back. I realized that death is a real option and possibility – regardless of how well you are trained and prepared. That it can happen to me as well. But at that time, I was still very young, adventurous, no kids waiting at home, and willing to test my limits at all costs. Further, this first real confrontation with death confirmed to Basti and me to continue with our speed climbing style: Climbing up light and fast and spending as little time in the death zone as possible. And, most of all, having the means to come down fast again – because most climbers do not die on the way up, but when descending slowly and completely exhausted.

My view about death, mortality, and suffering changed further over time. It was not so much the unknown dead climbers buried in the snow from previous expeditions who changed my perspective. Instead it was the weeks and months spent in Basecamps in Nepal, Pakistan, and China; in regions of extreme isolation and poverty lacking basic infrastructure and services such as hospitals, other forms of medical care, sanitation, food, and clean water. We had children coming to Basecamp with severe burns from the explosions of gas lamps in their parents' huts, with broken bones from falls or others accidents. These were moments when I started to really think about the finiteness about life and my existence. When something happened on these mountains you are most likely on your own – just like many of these families. You cannot call 911 and expect to be driven by an ambulance to the next hospital where a well-trained surgeon and his team await you. And you cannot count on a helicopter rescue team like in the Alps. With the thin air at 7500m helicopters – if there are any around – cannot hover to pick up injured climbers and bring them back to safety. You are on your own. And worse, you might die on your own. Facing this isolation and material poverty, and understanding how easily you can die in these mountains really started to change my view about life, mortality, and what really mattered to me.

But it was also the sudden deaths of people who you knew and who were close to you which changed further my view about mortality and suffering over time. In 2006 Basti's brother Tobi Haag had a fatal 800m fall from the Aguille D'Argentiere summit in Chamonix. In 2009, Matthias Robl, a very good friend of mine and climbing partner at the Mustagh Ata died in a climbing accident. In the same year Cristina Castagna died on her descent of the Broad Peak summit. A couple of nights before her death we had drinks together and joked who would be faster on the summit, as Basti and I planned a speed descent of Broad Peak from Basecamp on the same day as Cristina would start her summit push from Camp 3. And in March 2012 Cedric Hählen, who joined me during my ascent of Broad Peak in 2009, went missing during the first winter ascent attempt of Hidden Peak (8080m). These deaths and the suffering I have seen amongst the locals in those remote regions surrounding the mountains we climbed, made me mature quickly.

And this maturity was much needed because the worst had yet to come. In 2012 the mountaineering world faced one of the worst tragedies that had happened on an 8000m mountain. In the early morning hours of September 23, a huge avalanche buried almost 30 climbers in their camps on Manaslu at around 6800m. Five climbing friends and myself camped in close proximity to the accident in our Camp 2 at 6400m. We were the first to arrive at the accident zone at around 4:20am, 20 minutes after the accident. We saw tents being completely destroyed, some climbers sitting around in their underwear without boots as they were surprised by the avalanche whilst sleeping. The average survival time in an avalanche is about 10–15 min. We switched into pure functioning mode and searched for more survivors. While it was extremely intense, I had fewer qualms. Due to my previous experiences with mortality, I had lost this sense of anxiety when it comes to dealing with death and dead people. Mortality had become a permanent companion.

Eleven climbers died that day on Manaslu. When we were back in Basecamp, our thoughts were with the injured and dead climbers and all their relatives. Only later I started thinking about how lucky we were with our decision to camp away from the usual campsites. I asked myself if death is predetermined; if I was really in control of my destiny; how quickly it all can be over; how much time and energy I have been wasting on unimportant things; and how little I have been cherishing this beautiful gift of just being alive – healthy and loved. I realized that I was not ready to die; that I still wanted some time to have kids and see them growing up. Facing all these dead bodies made me realize what really mattered in my life. It was a profound reality and values check.

For a while after Peru and Mustagh Ata we had this tradition of returning home with great euphoria to have made it and to be still alive; after Manaslu 2012 I came back from the expedition much calmer. I felt more serene and tranquil. Many of the problems at work or at home which would have stressed me in the past didn't even seem like problems anymore. For example, when my son had a febrile seizure, my wife called me in tears at work and insisted to come home immediately. While the neighbors and grandparents were all distraught and distressed waiting around my house when I arrived home, I felt strangely calm. Don't get me wrong – I love my son; but I knew that it was not a life-threatening situation, that we had a hospital in close proximity, and that the doctor who was with my son knew his job.

And then came 2014 and our Double Eight attempt to climb Shisha Pangma (8027m) and the Cho Oyu (8188m) in 7 days without oxygen. The distance of 170km between the two Basecamps we wanted to cover by riding on mountain bikes and by running. The team on the final summit day to Shisha Pangma included Basti, Andrea Zambaldi, Ueli Steck, and Martin Maier. In the morning of September 23 we started our speed ascent attempt on the Shisha Pangma. About 100 altitude meters below the summit an avalanche killed Basti and Andrea. Martin survived with severe injuries. Losing climbing partners of your own rope team was extremely hurtful. Losing Basti was like losing a part of me on that mountain. He was more than a friend. He was an extension of me.

His death showed me how wrongly I have been defining this notion of heroism. We always look up to those who survive and forget the many great climbers and athletes that did not make it back. For me there are no heroes – some of us are just less lucky or predestined by their destiny than others. I have been asked many times before and after the accident of Basti, if it is worth dying for what we have been doing on these mountains. Basti always turned this question around and asked if it is worth living for. And just like him, I can only say yes, absolutely! Despite the risks and losses of close friends and climbing partners, I feel that mountaineering is my calling. This is where I face my limits and my thresholds, where I gain my serenity and refill my joy for life. Thanks to those experiences, today I live every day the fullest, as if it was my last.

Photo 6.1 *A massive avalanche coming down from the world's second highest mountain K2 (8611 m). We made this picture while climbing Broad Peak (8051m), another 8000m peak right next to K2 in Pakistan.*

Photo 6.2 *During our daily work out in bad weather conditions on Manaslu (8163m). We start from Basecamp (4900m) and march up to Camp 1 (6000m) escaping the cabin fever which comes quickly when being imprisoned in Basecamp by bad weather conditions.*

DEATH AWARENESS, DEATH, AND MORTALITY AT THE WORKPLACE AND BEYOND

Just like Ben and other extreme athletes, for many professionals death is a daily companion inside and outside of their workplace. Fire fighters, police officers, and members of the armed forces are usually the ones who come first to mind in such a context. But there is a long list of other professions in which individuals are regularly putting their own lives at risk including logging, the structural iron and steel construction sector, mining, high sea fishing, and the hazardous waste industry.[1] And one must not forget the many company leaders and decision makers who work on average 65 hours a week; often under extreme pressures and stress, and at a great risk to their personal health.[2] Scholars have pointed out the well documented and significant relationship between 'various measures of job strain and cardiovascular mortality'.[3] The deaths of Charlie Bell (former CEO of McDonalds) at age 60 and Ranjan Das (former CEO of SAP India) at age 42 are illustrative of how the biggest health risk to executives is heart attacks.[4]

Aside these professions in which individuals are personally facing death or near death experiences, there are professions in which individuals frequently face death vicariously by dealing with the death or near death of others. Such professions include hospital staff, nursing home employees, coroners, and undertakers. Finally, and regardless of the profession, research in personality and life-span developmental psychology has shown how aging plays a significant role when it comes to developing an awareness of one's own death and mortality.[5] Yet, despite the evidence that death awareness is an integral part of the aging process, and despite that there are numerous professions and businesses in which death and mortality play salient roles in the daily routines of their decision makers and employees, organizational scholars have rarely addressed and explored the role of death awareness, death, and mortality in organizational life.[6]

Much of the research about death awareness and mortality has been conducted in the fields of social sciences and humanities. From early on in history philosophers have explored the question of death and mortality. Heidegger and Sartre pointed at the 'anxiety, dread, and fear that people experience when they become aware of their own mortality'.[7] This awareness has been defined as 'a psychological state in which people are conscious of their mortality'.[8] The American anthropologist Ernest Becker's Pulitzer award winning book *The Denial of Death* is one of the most extensive and influential scholarly works about death awareness and mortality. Becker argues that humans' mental capability to think about themselves in abstract terms, and to contemplate themselves in hypothetical situations in the past, present, and future, allows them to become aware of the inevitability of their own death. And just as Ben describes his confrontation with his own mortality as brutal and somewhat scary, the awareness of our unavoidable finiteness can initially create fear and terror within us. According to Becker, the 'idea of death, the fear of it, haunts the human animal like nothing else […] Of all things that move man, one of the principal ones is his terror of death.'[9]

In the late 1980s scholars extended Becker's notion of terror of death and introduced a terror management theory of self-esteem and cultural worldviews.[10] According to these theorists most humans grow up in societies and work in organizational settings with cultural worldviews that are characterized by certain sets of values, beliefs, norms, and standards. Examples of worldviews can be Christian Theism, Atheism, Humanism, Existentialism, and many other religious and nonreligious views of the world that help us to explain and make sense of the world and how to live our lives. The more humans socialize and adhere to a particular cultural worldview, the stronger is their sense of purpose and belonging, and the more they feel protected against the fear of annihilation and the terror of death.[11] The adherence to a cultural system can strengthen an individual's belief in literal and/or symbolic immortality.[12] Literal immortality is often used in religious teachings whereby the soul or another non-corporeal aspect of an individual will transcend into an afterlife. Symbolic immortality refers to any aspect that 'endures over time and beyond individual death'.[13] Symbols of immortality can range from an office tower or street with one's name on it (e.g. Rockerfeller Center, Washington Avenue) to one's published books or music, or to one's unique athletic achievements. Extreme athlete Felix Baumgartner considered his base jump from the Christ the Redeemer statue at the summit of Mount Corcovado in Rio de Janeiro his most important jump in his life because it transformed him 'from being a nobody into become a somebody'[14] – a somebody the world is talking about, a somebody the world would always remember.

Within the field of personality and life-span development scholars propose a different perspective of death awareness and mortality. Key scholars such as the German-American developmental psychologist Erik Erikson – well known for his proposition of eight psychological stages of life and their corresponding development crises[15] – argues that when reaching midlife people become increasingly aware of death. This awareness leads to a crisis and reflections about how satisfied or regretful one is with one's life,[16] and about contributing to the next generation (generativity) or ceasing to be a productive member of society (stagnation). 'Those who succumb to this crisis experience despair, continuing to fear and dread death. Those who overcome this crisis experience ego integrity, finding coherence and meaning in their lives and accepting death'.[17] In the case of Ben, over time his reflections about mortality led him to a profound reality and values check-up, and to readjusting his priorities accordingly. Thus, it is not only sudden life-threatening or near death experiences that change one's view about death and mortality. The older adults get, the more comfortable they are with their own mortality and with what truly matters to them.[18]

WHEN AND HOW DEATH BECOMES SALIENT TO EMPLOYEES IN ORGANIZATIONAL SETTINGS

Whichever of those two key arguments or perspectives about death awareness and mortality one wants to adopt, both have relevance and implications for the workplace. Death awareness or mortality cues in organizational settings can be triggered by different events 'that occur in a bounded time period and place'.[19] The source of the mortality cue can be found inside or outside the organization. It can be of an acute or chronic nature that personally involves, or vicariously affects, the manager or employee. The different combinations of source of mortality cues, their frequency and duration, and the relevance of them to the employee can influence his or her death anxiety and death reflection. Professionals exposed personally on a regular basis on or off the job to life threatening situations and events tend to have relatively little death anxiety and moderate to intense death reflections. A soldier patrolling every day or night the streets of a war-torn place like Kabul will eventually have learnt to cope with the city's constant dangers just like Apple co-founder Steve Jobs had learnt to come to terms with his life threating pancreatic cancer disease, even though the thoughts of dying might have frequently crossed both their minds.

Professionals who experience short-lived or momentary life-threatening situations inside or outside the organization that affect them personally tend to show moderate to strong death anxiety and few death reflections. This could be a near fatal accident inside or outside the workplace like in the case of Douglas Conant, former CEO of Campbell Soup Company. He described his car accident in which he broke ten ribs and severely damaged several internal organs as his 'most harrowing experience' of his life.[20] Professionals who are indirectly confronted with recurring and lasting (near) death events inside or outside of the workplace tend to demonstrate little death anxiety and moderate death reflections. Nurses and doctors in hospitals often use humor to cope with the death of patients or put their emotions aside 'because there are other patients waiting for you.'[21]

And finally, professionals who are involved in intermittent situations at the workplace or outside the organization, and that are dangerous or fatal to others to which these professionals have some emotional proximity, tend to show moderate death anxiety and few death reflections.[22] Examples of this last combination at the workplace are the suicides of Carsten Schloter (CEO of Swisscom) and Pierre Wahtier (VP Finance, Zuerich Insurance) in 2013, or the fatal plane accident of Total's CEO Christophe de Margerie in 2014, and their sudden deaths' impact on employees and managers at their respective companies; examples of this last combination outside the workplace are the sudden death of a close relative in the family – like in the case in the case of Sheryl Sandberg (COO of Facebook) whose husband died in an accident at the gym in 2015. Sandberg's Facebook essay that she published after the death of her husband illustrates some of the implications the death of individuals inside and outside of an organization can have on managers and decision makers.

THE IMPLICATIONS OF DEATH ANXIETY AND DEATH REFLECTION ON EMPLOYEES' BEHAVIORS

Depending on the different types of mortality clues, decision makers and employees show different tendencies when it comes to their feelings of apprehending death and their reflections about death and mortality. These feelings and reflections can have destructive implications for managers and their employees' motivation. In 1989 all members of the top two management levels of the Norwegian maritime industry group Wilh. Wilhelmnsen died in a plane crash. When Ingar Skaug took over the leadership of the company 3 months after the accident he faced employees who were 'trapped in mourning, unable to focus and make decisions. The offices and plants were disheveled and disorganized. It was an organization paralyzed by grief'.[23] While Skaug was able to reengage his employees and turn around the company, managers and employees experiencing a strong or enduring sense of death anxiety tend to withdraw from work. Anxiety can be a significant stress factor and for employees to protect themselves from this overwhelming pressure and strain, they do not show up at work or show sluggish behaviors when they are at their workplace.[24]

But death awareness can also produce positive effects on employees' motivation – or as Austrian philosopher Wittgenstein put it – only death gives life its meaning.[25] They can be particularly constructive and beneficial when the outcomes emerge from reflections about mortality and death rather than death anxiety.[26] For Ben the death of climbing friends was an eye opener for him. His reflections about death enabled him to understand what really mattered to him in life. For Steve Jobs death was life's change agent, 'very likely the single best invention of life'. Jobs' experiences of living with pancreatic cancer led him to appeal to students at the University of Stanford to not waste their lives 'living someone else's life' and instead to 'have the courage to follow your heart and intuition'.[27] For SAP's Chief executive Bill McDermott his life's changing moment was his accident in 2015, when he slipped on the stairs one night with a glass in his hand. McDermott suffered facial fractures, lost one eye, and nearly bled to death. Looking back the businessman explains how this near death experience had changed his life and his perspective: I was always in the moment before the accident but there's a depth and a range to life when you realize you almost didn't have one. You just feel things at a very deep human level and there is a greater appreciation for every encounter. I love being in service to other people.[28] Whether it is athletes or business people, experiences and reflections about death can lead to a critical self-analysis about an individual's purpose or personal mission statement, and the values and beliefs that shape one's worldview; in short it is a means to get a better idea what really matters in one's life.

McDermott's serving attitude illustrates how death reflections can influence individuals' mindsets and 'broaden their focus of attention beyond their own narrow career goals toward a consideration of helping others and doing good'.[29] Throughout the aging process these death reflections increase and death anxiety decreases. Age or aging in this context refers not only to the biological aging but also to the symbolic aging processes such as advancing career stages, occupational tenure, and retirement planning programs. These symbols can 'strengthen employees' tendencies to reflect on death by serving as reminders of time passed and by highlighting that time left is finite and decreasing'.[30] With age individuals become increasingly emotionally stable and thorough, allowing them to look at death and mortality more pragmatically and less worryingly. Consequently, aging employees tend to be more and more interested and engaged in altruistic and generative activities at the workplace. They show greater empathy and responsibility toward others. They want to contribute to the success of colleagues and subordinates, and give something back to their organization or the community'.[31] A recent example of decision makers illustrating such behavioral trends is Jack Ma, the former CEO of the Chinese e-commerce group Alibaba. Ma stepped down in September 2018 declaring to follow in the footsteps of Bill Gates, Warren Buffet, and Carlos Slim by spending more of his time and fortune on philanthropy.[32] Altruistic and generative actions by employees on the job work particularly well when their jobs are meaningful to them and they have the autonomy and flexibility to tailor their jobs according to their altruistic interests. For business leaders this requires an understanding of others and what they consider as meaningful. And to understand others starts by understanding oneself first. And that's where greater awareness and understanding of one's finiteness and mortality can play an essential role.

KEY ARGUMENTS AND TAKEAWAYS:

- Be aware and understand that organizational boundaries do not prevent (near) death experiences off the job from influencing individuals' performances on the job. Don't waste time and money on coaching or training when counselling employees is what is needed to change an individual's drop in performance.
- When dealing with death experiences or death awareness, minimize death anxiety and focus on death reflections. The latter has positive consequences for employees' self-awareness, motivation, and generative behaviors.
- Use and benefit from individual altruistic attitudes and behaviors that develop through death reflections by channeling them through organizational processes such as mentoring and sponsoring programs. Younger and less experienced employees and managers can greatly benefit from these generative behaviors.
- Be aware that intense death anxiety amongst employees can influence negatively the employee's performance or lead to temporary to permanent withdrawal from the job. This has implications on absenteeism rates and labor turnover.
- Death reflections are effective means for reality check ups. They help you realize what really matters in life. Exercises[33] focusing on mortality and death awareness and reflection can be integrated in the self-development process.

NOTES

1 Stebbins, S. Comen, E. and Stockdale, C. 2018. Workplace fatalities: 25 most dangerous jobs in America. *USA Today*, January 9. At https://eu.usatoday.com/story/money/careers/2018/01/09/workplace-fatalities-25-most-dangerous-jobs-america/1002500001/

2 Pullen, J. 2015. This is the secret way CEOs stay ultra-productive. *Time*. At http://time.com/4076563/ceos-productivity/

3 Wright, T. and Wright, Z. 2002. Organizational researcher values, ethical responsibility, and the committed to participant research perspective. *Journal of Management Inquiry*, 11(2), page 178.

4 Fasula, R. 2013. CEOs and heart disease. *The CEO Magazine*. At http://media.the-ceo-magazine.com/guest/ceos-and-heart-disease-0

5 Stewart, A. and Ostrove, J. 1998. Women's personality in middle age: Gender, history, and midcourse corrections. *American Psychologist*, 53(11), 1185–1194.

6 Grant, A. and Wade-Benzoni, K. 2009. The hot and cool of death awareness at work: Mortality cues, aging, and self-protective and prosocial motivations. *Academy of Management Review*, 34(4), 600–622.

7 Grant, A. and Wade-Benzoni, K. 2009. The hot and cool of death awareness at work: Mortality cues, aging, and self-protective and prosocial motivations. *Academy of Management Review*, 34(4), page 602.

8 Grant, A. and Wade-Benzoni, K. 2009. The hot and cool of death awareness at work: Mortality cues, aging, and self-protective and prosocial motivations. *Academy of Management Review*, 34(4), page 602.

9 Becker, E. 1973. *The denial of death*. New York: Simon and Schuster, pp. ix and 11.

10 See Greenberg, J., Pyszczynski, T. and Solomon, S. 1986. The causes and consequences of a need for self-esteem: A terror management theory. In R. F. Baumeister (Ed.), *Public self and private self* (pp. 189–212). New York, NY: Springer-Verlag; Rosenblatt, A., Greenberg, J., Solomon, S., Pyszczynski, T. and Lyon, D. 1989. Evidence for terror management theory I: The effects of mortality salience on reactions to those who violate or uphold cultural values. *Journal of Personality and Social Psychology*, 57(4), 681–690; Greenberg, J., Pyszczynski, T., Solomon, S. and Rosenblatt, A. 1990. Evidence for terror management theory II: The effects of mortality salience on reactions to those who threaten or bolster the cultural worldview. *Journal of Personality and Social Psychology*, 58(2), 308–318.

11 Stein, J. and Cropanzano, R. 2011. Death awareness and organizational behavior. *Journal of Organizational Behavior*, 32, 1189–1193.

12 Cicirelli, V. 2002. Fear of death in older adults: Predictions from terror management theory. *Journal of Gerontology: Psychological Sciences*, 57B(4), 358–366.

13 Cicirelli, V. 2002. Fear of death in older adults: Predictions from terror management theory. *Journal of Gerontology: Psychological Sciences*, 57B(4), page 359.

14 Televised interview with Markus Lanz on October 17, 2013. At https://www.youtube.com/watch?v=pTSzw4xac14

15 See Erikson, E. 1982. *The life cycle completed.* New York: Norton.

16 Grant, A. and Wade-Benzoni, K. 2009. The hot and cool of death awareness at work: Mortality cues, aging, and self-protective and prosocial motivations. *Academy of Management Review*, 34(4), page 605.

17 Grant, A. and Wade Benzoni, K. 2009. The hot and cool of death awareness at work: Mortality cues, aging, and self protective and prosocial motivations. *Academy of Management Review*, 34(4), page 605.

18 Fortner, B., Neimeyer, R. and Rybarczyk, B. 2000. Correlates of death anxiety in older adults: A comprehensive review. In A. Tomer (Ed.), *Death attitudes and the older adult: Theories, concepts, and applications* (pp. 95–108). Philadelphia, PA: Taylor & Francis.

19 Grant, A. and Wade-Benzoni, K. 2009. The hot and cool of death awareness at work: Mortality cues, aging, and self-protective and prosocial motivations. *Academy of Management Review*, 34(4), page 606.

20 Conant, D. 2017. *Leadership lessons from a near-fatal car accident.* At https://conantleadership.com/leadership-lessons-from-a-near-fatal-car-accident/

21 Domrose, C. 2011. *Good grief: Nurses cope with patient deaths.* At https://www.nurse.com/blog/2011/02/21/good-grief-nurses-cope-with-patient-deaths/

22 Grant, A. and Wade-Benzoni, K. 2009. The hot and cool of death awareness at work: Mortality cues, aging, and self-protective and prosocial motivations. *Academy of Management Review*, 34(4), 600–622.

23 Tardanico, S. 2012. Entire management team killed: A CEO's turnaround story. *Forbes.* At https://www.forbes.com/sites/susantardanico/2012/03/28/entire-management-team-killed-a-ceos-turnaround-story/#5bea1ae64d61

24 Byron, K. and Peterson, S. 2002. The impact of a large scale traumatic event on individual and organizational outcomes: Exploring employee and company reactions to September 11, 2001. *Journal of Organizational Behavior*, 23(8), 895–910.

25 Beale, J. 2018. Wittgenstein's confessions. *New York Times*. At https://www.nytimes.com/2018/09/18/opinion/wittgensteins-confession-philosophy.html

26 Grant, A. and Wade-Benzoni, K. 2009. The hot and cool of death awareness at work: Mortality cues, aging, and self-protective and prosocial motivations. *Academy of Management Review*, 34(4), page 614.

27 Jobs, S. 2011. Steve Jobs: Death is very likely the single best invention of life. *The Guardian*. At https://www.theguardian.com/technology/2011/oct/06/steve-jobs-pancreas-cancer

28 Taylor, C. 2017. McDermott has world domination in his sights after near-death experience. *Irish Times*. At https://www.irishtimes.com/business/technology/mcdermott-has-world-domination-in-his-sights-after-near-death-experience-1.3267307

29 Grant, A. and Wade-Benzoni, K. 2009. The hot and cool of death awareness at work: Mortality cues, aging, and self-protective and prosocial motivations. *Academy of Management Review*, 34(4), page 613.

30 Grant, A. and Wade-Benzoni, K. 2009. The hot and cool of death awareness at work: Mortality cues, aging, and self-protective and prosocial motivations. *Academy of Management Review*, 34(4), page 610.

31 Cicirelli, V. 2002. Fear of death in older adults: Predictions from terror management theory. *Journal of Gerontology: Psychological Sciences*, 57B(4), 358–366.

32 Chen, L. and Mackenzie, T. 2018. Billionaire Jack Ma prepares for life after Alibaba. *Bloomberg*. At https://www.bloomberg.com/news/articles/2018-09-06/billionaire-jack-ma-prepares-for-life-after-alibaba

33 Exercise: Imagine you are dead. It is your funeral. Imagine that the people who mattered the most to you have five minutes to speak. What did they most appreciate about you? What did your life mean to them? What impact did it have? What have they lost with your passing? Write these words down as though you were that person. This gets you started to determine what really matters and what you value. It helps to determine what would have to change in your life in order to create these outcomes.

CHAPTER SEVEN

About suffering

SUBTEXT: One day, in retrospect, the years of struggle will strike you as the most beautiful[1]

My climbing partner Basti used to say that the physical suffering leads to a mental liberation. And in many situations, this is how I have felt. When I push my body to my physical limits – and sometimes beyond – then often I feel a sense of mental liberation or freeing afterwards. Despite the physical exhaustion I feel a deep contentment and serenity. In particular in situations when my climbing partners and I have returned from a summit ascent. When all the tensions are gone, and we all have made it back to Basecamp in one piece. My mountaineering projects and expeditions are neither about first or second prizes, nor gold or silver medals. What thrives and pushes me through the suffering during the projects but also in many of the preparation and training sessions is most often the urge for this very personal gratification and inner peacefulness.

The physical exhaustion in daily training sessions gives me the mental balance so important in my hectic other lives as the leader of a global (mountain) sporting goods company and father of three small children. The physical efforts in daily training routines help me to step out temporarily from the daily matrices in which we are stuck – often reigned by mountains of emails and ringing cellphones. Getting up very early in the morning for 2–3 hours of training sessions – regardless how hard they are – provides me my daily dose of disconnection. The physical suffering during those sessions often feels like a mental cleansing (and when a training session follows a night out with some old climbing friends, it equally provides the literal, physical cleaning). The physical pain reduces the thinking to the here and now, helping me to clear my mind. And I can almost literally sweat out any bottled up frustrations or any other negative emotions.

But most of these aspects of physical suffering are just side-effects. The key of all the suffering is finding and pushing my limits. I am trying to go step by step beyond these limits and extend my physical threshold. Pushing the physical limits can reduce the physical suffering. The more you push the threshold the later the suffering starts or at least your mind is better prepared for coping with the suffering. But to achieve this effect means tailoring the training efforts toward the goal or objectives. Pushing the limits helps me to develop greater self-confidence and resilience. And with greater self-confidence and resilience I gain the faith to push my limits further again. It becomes a dynamic process of self-development at a physical and mental level.

This process started for me as early as a teenager training cross-country skiing. Just like in many other endurance sports, talent was important, but discipline, commitment, and hard work were equally relevant to succeed in cross-country skiing. I had a coach who taught me that above all these attributes 'Leidensfähigkeit' was the most salient one – the capability of suffering or the ability to endure suffering. Many times my experiences confirmed his saying that you cannot avoid pain, but you can train and control for how much and how long you can endure the pain. Regardless of how much you train or how often you climb up a mountain, the pain will hit you eventually. And you cannot make the pain disappear or escape from it unless you give up. But you can train how well you endure the pain.

This takes a lot of self-discipline and self-critique. Just like everybody else, I experience days I do not want to get up and train, or situations in which I just want to turn around on a mountain run at 3am in the pitch dark and freezing cold. You have to be very honest with yourself in such situations. Is the pain really a serious warning signal that you reached your absolute limit? Is it really a question of ability? Or is it purely a question of motivation and willpower? Most often I do not allow any thought for the option of giving up – regardless of how tempting the alternatives might be. I know I would feel worse afterwards than how I feel in the very moment of doubt. I know that any training or preparation I do is like paying money into a savings account. Only when you saved enough money you can buy a house; and only the hours of hard training you put in will eventually bring you to the summit.

The physical suffering nourishes your willpower. And it is the willpower that makes you overcome mental suffering such as self-doubt, distress, or fright. Despite the common saying 'Willpower can move mountains', I feel that mental suffering and the importance of willpower are often underestimated. We tend to focus on the physical aspects. From experience, I believe this is wrong. My worst suffering on ascending an 8000m peak has never been the physical suffering. Despite the physical pain and exhaustion, I see progress – regardless how slow. I can see that I am coming closer to the summit. There is progress and movement. The worst suffering is when there is no movement or progress. When you are stuck in a steep face – no way up, down, or sideways. No movement, no progress – just like so many times in Basecamp. You are stuck. Stuck together with others for weeks in tents and waiting for the rain or snow to stop. Everything is soaking wet and nothing dries. You have too much time on hands. You start to question the objective of the tour, your abilities, the abilities of the others. And eventually your confidence in yourself and the others shrinks. You can get mentally really low in such situations. That is when you have to really dig deep into your mind to be very clear and honest to yourself about why you are doing all this and for what you are suffering. And somehow you have to get moving again. On Manaslu in 2012 we were stuck for days in Basecamp due to a snow whiteout. We addressed the rising mental tensions within the team by climbing every day 1000 altitude meters up and down in deep snow and almost zero visibility. The physical exhaustion helped us to get mentally stronger. After a week we could walk these 1000m blindfolded. We slept better, and the daily dull rice dish in the evening after a hard day's work tasted also much better.

Other ways that have helped me to better cope with the mental and the physical suffering on my tours are the setting of clear goals and objectives. Being fully aware of what is the goal makes the suffering easier to endure. Knowing what's coming helps to prepare your mind and mental state. In 2018, when I speed ascended the Iranian Damavand (5671m) straight from the Caspian Sea, I knew after an extremely exhausting bike ride that there was still a run in high altitude to come. This awareness did not make the run physically any easier, but my mind was prepared for it and I endured the suffering much better. In contrast, when somebody keeps telling me that the finish line is coming up soon but without any detailed times or distances, then this uncertainty becomes first and foremost a challenge of the mind.

With the clear goals being set comes the definition of success that influences how I cope better with the suffering. When it comes to an 8000m summit and the conditions are good – externally in terms of temperature, snow, or wind, and internally in terms of physical fitness and acclimatization – then success can only be the summit and coming back down in one piece. And the suffering is adapted to that definition of success. But if the external or internal conditions are not at their optimum – if there is a whiteout, heavy snow fall, fog, or I have been sick – then success is redefined and the acceptable levels of suffering are lowered. In the world of speed mountaineering and mountaineering in general, success and its meaning to the climbers can change rapidly, and with this change vary the levels of acceptable or required suffering.

What is acceptable and not in terms of effort and the accompanying suffering depends also on the reward that comes with those exertions and pains. This can be a nice and cold beer or a beautiful skiing descent after an exhausting ascend, or a tour in beautiful surroundings – after all, there is nothing more beautiful than experiencing a sunrise in complete solitude on a mountain – at least to me. Tailoring or matching your physical suffering to goals, success, and rewards requires a very good understanding of your body. At some point, I was at a stage where training and constantly pushing of limits became compulsory and obsessive. Today I understand that in those days I sometimes did more harm to my body than good. Thus, you always need to control and balance your temptations of giving up too early versus letting go too late.

In many such situations I was lucky to have had a partner with me who either pushed me further when our limits could still be expanded, or held me back when our limits were fully reached. The German term for such a person is 'Leidensgefährte' or a comrade in suffering. Similar to the notion of fear, sharing the suffering with a comrade in suffering means enduring half of the pain and agony. And that can really make a difference. After all, none of us likes to suffer unless it is for a very good reason.

Photo 7.1 *Totally exhausted. Returning back to Broad Peak Basecamp after a 48 hours non-stop speed push from Basecamp (4800m) to Broad Peak pre-summit (8021m). Things went out of control after having lost too much time and energy breaking trail in horrible snow conditions all the way up to the pre-summit. Basti had problems making his way down and our friend Cristina Castagna had a deadly fall off the summit ridge of Broad Peak. We had lost not only more than 10kg weight within these 48 hours, but we also had experienced our absolute limits.*

Photo 7.2 *Even Basecamp can become a challenge and nightmare: A group of mountaineers leaving Broad Peak Basecamp after days and weeks of bad weather.*

Photo 7.3 *Daily routine: Digging out our tents every couple of hours during 12 days non-stop heavy snow falls at Manaslu (8163m). A mental nightmare that brought us close to madness.*

PHYSICAL AND MENTAL SUFFERING AT THE WORKPLACE

Physical and mental suffering is not just a phenomenon to be found in extreme sports or in organizations operating in extreme conditions. Today it is in particular the mental suffering that is widely spread throughout most organizations, professions, age groups, and organizational levels. Mental suffering can have many causes or forms ranging from anxiety to fright, depression, stress, and burnout. Rates for burnout and other forms of mental suffering have been reported to be up to 62 percent amongst professionals and workers.[2] The occupational group that is mostly affected by these symptoms is the one of middle managers. Middle managers usually find themselves in a contradictory class location by which they are caught in the middle and regularly have to absorb the opposing demands from their superiors and subordinates. 'Middle managers often have to enforce strategic policies from the top— ones they didn't develop—on subordinates who might object to those new policies'. Consequently, middle managers very frequently 'get flak from above and below'.[3]

Organization scholars and the business press have largely focused their studies and reports on the negative implications for managers and employees when it comes to mental and physical suffering at the workplace. Yet amongst those writers who have highlighted the many negative effects of physical and mental pain and suffering, there are some authors who simultaneously suggest that forms of suffering such as stress are normal and have their benefits.[4] According to the transactional theory of stress,[5]

> stress may have negative or positive implications for the individual depending on how the demands that evoke the stress process are believed to affect personal growth, development, and well-being – demands can be appraised as benign, harmful, or threatening, or they can be appraised as a challenge or opportunity.[6]

And just like there is some good stress,[7] Ben's experiences suggest that there can be some good suffering, or at least that there can be something good in suffering. Ben has explained how suffering for a particular goal and reason creates a number of positive effects for him.

FINDING CONTENTMENT AND SERENITY

Some of these positive effects have been described by Ben as freeing himself from negative emotions and tensions and reaching a sense of contentment and serenity. This is partly due to brain chemicals – dopamine, serotonin, oxytocin, and endorphins – that are activated and released in the physical activity that eventually get Ben into a state of physical suffering. Dopamine is felt as 'engagement, excitement, creativity, and a desire to investigate and make meaning out of the world'.[8] Serotonin plays an important role in mood regulation. Lower levels of this neurotransmitter are associated with feelings of depression,[9] whereas increased levels help coping with adversity.[10] Oxytocin has been described as the love molecule and is considered 'the chemical foundation for trusting others'.[11] Endorphins not only help to relieve pain but produce a feeling of pleasure and natural high. Runners often refer to this chemical's effect as a 'runner's high' during longer runs. Considering the four neurochemicals' cocktail of positive effects on the body and mind, it does not come as a surprise that they have been shown to also affect positively employees' productivity at the workplace.[12] In other words, certain stress levels or other forms of suffering at the workplace can help managers and employees to experience a 'worker's high'.

DISCONNECTING

Ben also explained how during periods of physical suffering he can clear his mind and become disconnected from the rest of the world. This effect could also be considered as a physiological consequence or bodily response to the suffering. Regardless whether it is a challenging training climb or stepping through deep snow at 8000m altitude – in such situations Ben's physical efforts and those of the mind are focused on the simple routine of putting one foot in front of another. This not only allows him to save the necessary energy that keeps him going, but also to switch off or to disconnect. In other words, physical suffering can put the body into an energy saving mode by reducing all brain activities to one thought. And as the mind allows only for one thought at a time, you purposefully inhibit or ignore any other thoughts that come to your mind.[13] Physical suffering can be considered as an active form of meditation because it forces the individual to immerse him or herself in the present – entering a state of thoughtless awareness.[14] The inattention to other thoughts can of course be achieved in many other ways. Bill Gates and Jeff Bezos, for example, unwind and relax washing up their families' dinner dishes every night.[15] For some readers this chore might be just another form of suffering – yet with the same positive effects.

STRENGTHENING WILLPOWER AND SELF-CONTROL

For Ben, suffering in his training and his projects is not only helping him to clear his head and free him from negative emotions but, more profoundly, suffering is helping him in his self-discovery, in finding his limits, and in his search for meaning and purpose. More and more business people engage purposely in physical suffering for those very same reasons – and often they choose extreme resistance sports such as long distance triathlons and ultramarathons as the means for their physical and mental suffering. Business leaders such as Rich Williams of Groupon participates in the 160km long Leadville 100 mountain running race, Michael Johnson of Herbalife is a known triathlon fanatic, while Francesco Casoli of Elica has been training for the 103km long Dolomites mountain running race.[16] These sporting events require many intense and lengthy training sessions. Thus, the top morning activity of successful business people before breakfast has become exercising.[17]

The physical exercising and suffering helps these business women and men to develop their willpower and self-control that are important in the process of finding and pushing their limits. Or as one former Inc. 500 CEO and long distance triathlete describes, you have to be a master of discipline and have a great deal of mental stamina and fortitude.[18] This mental strength or willpower has been described as the energy resource that influences self-control. Though the term willpower has traditionally been used metaphorically, it has been shown that willpower has a physical base in form of glucose, a chemical that transmits energy in the bloodstream of the human body to the brain and muscles.[19] Willpower functions like a muscle. And as with other muscles, it can be strengthened through training and fatigued with overuse. Little to no willpower or ego depletion leads to poor self-control.

Self-control has been described as the control over one's behavior and emotions. Self-control is about resisting inducements and remaining focused and persistent on a task despite distractions and the temptation of instant pleasure[20]. American psychologist Walter Mischel's famous marshmallow experiment[21] illustrates how self-control is about delaying gratification or delay discounting.[22] One forgoes an immediate enjoyment for a deferred but more desirable reward. In this experiment in the late 1960s, Mischel seated preschool-age children alone at a table with a marshmallow in front of them. The children were instructed by an adult that they could ring with a bell for the adult to come back and then eat the marshmallow; or they could wait until the adult returned voluntarily and then be rewarded with another marshmallow. Some children could not wait more than a minute (low delayers) whereas others were able to wait up to 20 minutes (high delayers). Based on their findings Mischel and his colleagues developed a 'hot and cool system' by which they explained why and when willpower and self-control succeed and fail. The cool system is cognitive and reflective in nature focusing on knowledge and rational thinking – "if I wait some time, I will get not only one but two marshmallows". The hot system is impulsive and emotional in nature, with quick and reflexive responses – "this marshmallow looks so tasty I have to have it now". Strong willpower and self-control is achieved when the cool system overrides the hot system.[23]

Therefore willpower and self-control are critical in decision-making processes. Low willpower and poor self-control can lead to decisions that 'are irrationally biased by logically irrelevant information, because people fail to recognize the irrelevance of certain factors. Some decision makers also prefer to avoid or postpone decisions when they are depleted'.[24] Thus, by training their willpower and self-control through high intensity physical exercising and suffering, Ben and business leaders not only push their limits in their sporting endeavors, but they also develop their decision-making competencies critical for their professional and personal lives. Mischel and studies following up his early works found that high delayers 'had achieved greater academic success, better health, and more positive relationships'.[25]

SUFFERING TO FIND MEANING AND MEANING TO CONTROL SUFFERING

Ben's experiences and the many business men and women training in resilience sports have illustrated that by pushing the physical limits, the physical and mental suffering can be delayed. Scholars such as the Viennese psychiatrist and neurologist Victor Frankl have demonstrated how physical and mental suffering can be controlled even further. In his key oeuvre 'Man's Search for Meaning'[26] Frankl describes his experiences as a Jewish prisoner in four different Nazi concentration camps in the 1940s. During that time, his wife was forced by the Gestapo to have an abortion before she and Frankl's mother were murdered in the gas chambers of Auschwitz. Frankl's father died of starvation and exhaustion in the Theresienstadt Ghetto in the Czech Republic.[27] Despite these terrible experiences and times of great physical and mental suffering, Frankl and other inmates were able to find meaning in their lives as prisoners. Some prisoners found meaning in people who awaited them outside the prison; people for whom it was worthwhile to endure the suffering. Frankl found his purpose in helping his fellow prisoners to create a meaning in life, not to give up, not to choose suicide as their way out. This meaning or purpose gave them the willpower and strength to endure their daily physical and mental suffering. Finding meaning made them far more resilient to suffering than those who did not.[28] When one knows the 'why' for his existence, he will be able to bear almost any 'how'[29]. Though pain was inevitable, suffering became optional and therefore controllable. Frankl recalls that 'everything can be taken from a man but one thing, the last of the human freedoms – to choose one's attitude in any given set circumstances, to choose one's own way'.[30]

Ben describes Frankl's search for meaning as digging really deep into his mind; to be very clear and honest to himself and the reason behind the actions that he chose and that made him suffer. While Frankl's suffering in the concentrations camps was inevitable and Ben's anguish deliberate, for both suffering has given them the means to discover meaning and values to their lives. As such, suffering becomes meaningful in itself, or as Frankl states: If there is a meaning in life at all, then there must a meaning in suffering. Suffering is an ineradicable part of life, even as fate and death. Without suffering and death human life cannot be complete.[31] Frankl's search for meaning provides an alternative approach to life for Ben and those who purposefully seek suffering in sports and other activities, from today's widespread pursuit of individual happiness.[32] Being clear about one's purpose and values provides contentment and self-confidence.[33] The active pursuit of experiencing happiness is its own barrier to achieving it. The more one tries to feel better and happier, the more dissatisfied one becomes 'as pursuing something only reinforces the fact that you lack it in the first place'.[34] Experiencing happiness cannot be pursued; it ensues. Experiences of happiness are unintended by-products of values[35]; and as experiences they are short lived when considering that the psychological present is about three seconds long.[36] In other words, experiences of happiness by themselves are nothing more than 'empty highs'.[37]

The life of Second Lieutenant Hiroo Onoda of the Japanese Imperial Army is illustrative of this conclusion. Onoda was hiding for 29 years in his jungle post on the island of Lubang in the Philippines despite the capitulation of the Japanese Empire at the end of World War II. Numerous attempts by the governments of Japan and the Philippines failed to convince him that the war was over and that he could return to Japan. He continued to follow his original order to fight and to never surrender. This order and his military code of honor (integrity, loyalty, and perseverance) gave Onoda the purpose and values to endure the physical and mental suffering that came with living for all these years in the jungle – many of which he spent in solitude because comrades either died or surrendered.[38]

When he was finally found and persuaded to return to Japan, his coming back felt to him like a culture shock. His initial enjoyment of being hailed as a national hero vanished quickly. Everything that meant something to him – the Empire and traditional Japanese values – had given way to materialism, consumption, and self-pursuits. He became disillusioned and started to question his very purpose that helped him to survive all the years in the Philippine jungle. Within a few years he left Japan disappointed and disheartened and moved to Brazil.[39]

SUFFERING AND RESILIENCE

Onoda and Frankl's experiences show how suffering and the search for meaning are interconnected and interdependent. Suffering can help to find meaning in one's life; and this meaning can help us to endure and somewhat control physical and mental suffering. This meaning gives us direction, persistence, and intensity. In other words, your purpose in life shows you your path; and the stronger you believe in your purpose the longer and harder you will try to follow this path. Thus, direction, persistence, and intensity are essential elements in one's motivation and are critical in attaining one's goals.[40] According to Frankl, 'what man actually needs is not a tensionless state but rather the striving and struggling for a worthwhile goal'[41]; or, as Ben says – there must be a good reason for my suffering. The better this reason or the more worthwhile the goal, the greater becomes the resilience to suffering.

More and more business men and women are searching and finding such a reason or goal in extreme endurance sports such as marathons and triathlons. And by doing so, they are training their resilience, their ability to bounce back from difficult and challenging experiences. This ability has become a key requirement in the selection of top executives.[42] However, although bouncing back is a key competence amongst successful top managers, it is rarely learnt on the job.[43] This is why companies might want to encourage employees to participate in activities outside the workplace with which they can strengthen and develop their resilience.

Finally, the increasing amount of business people taking on high resilience activities off the job might simply be an escape from a workplace and work that have become less and less meaningful in their lives. For organizations to sustain competitiveness, they might want to revise what organizational changes can create a workplace in which managers and employees are 'purpose driven and value led'[44]; a workplace where employees are given a clear direction and a strong sense of purpose and belonging.

KEY ARGUMENTS AND TAKEAWAYS:

- Get the right level of stress. It can activate a neurochemical cocktail which creates a sense of contentment and serenity or a worker's high.
- Consider using activities which create some physical suffering as a means to clear your mind when you need time to disconnect and switch off. Similar to meditation, such activities can help you to immerse yourself in the present entering a state of thoughtless awareness.
- Train your willpower through high intensity physical exercising to reach certain levels of physical suffering. Willpower is important in the process of finding and pushing your limits and helps you to develop your mental stamina and fortitude. Greater self-control positively influences your decision making in your professional and personal lives.
- It is not about how to stop suffering. Understand why you suffer. Having a clear purpose and set of values in life will help you to endure and control your suffering.
- Encourage employees to participate in activities outside the workplace with which they can strengthen and develop their resilience. Though bouncing back is a key competence amongst successful top managers, it is rarely learnt on the job.

NOTES

1 Sigmund Freud Letter to Carl Jung, September 19, 1907.
2 Valcour, M. 2016. Beating burnout. *Harvard Business Review*, November, 98–101.
3 Lam, B. 2015. The secret suffering of the middle manager. *The Atlantic*. August 27. At https://www.theatlantic.com/business/archive/2015/08/middle-managers-stress-depression/402193/

4 See McKee, A. 2018. *How to be happy at work.* Cambridge, MA: Harvard Business Press; Cavanaugh, M., Boswell, W., Roehling, M. and Boudreau, J. 2000. An empirical examination of self-reported work stress among U.S. managers. *The Journal of Applied Psychology,* 85(1), 65–74.

5 Lazarus, R. and Folkman, S. 1984. *Stress, appraisal, and coping.* New York, NY: Springer.

6 Le Pine, M., Zhang, Y., Crawford, E. and Rich, B. 2016. Turning their pain to gain: Charismatic leader influence on follower stress appraisal and job performance. *Academy of Management Journal,* 59(3), page 1036.

7 McKee, A. 2018. *How to be happy at work.* Cambridge, MA: Harvard Business Press.

8 Kotler, S. 2014. *The rise of superman.* New York: HarperCollins, page 66–67.

9 Nolen-Hoeksema, S. Fredrickson, B., Loftus, G. and Wagenaar, W. 2009. *Atkinson and Hilgard's introduction to psychology.* Andover, UK: Cengage Learning, page 42.

10 Kotler, S. 2014. *The rise of superman.* New York: HarperCollins, page 67.

11 Zak, P. 2013. The top 10 ways to boost good feelings. *Psychology Today.* At https://www.psychologytoday.com/intl/blog/the-moral-molecule/201311/the-top-10-ways-boost-good-feelings

12 See Kotler, S. and Wheal, J. 2017. *Stealing fire.* New York: HarperCollins.

13 Sacchet, M., La Plante, R. Wan, Q., Pritchett, D., Lee, A., Hämäläinen, M., Moore, C., Kerr, C. and Jones, S. 2015. Attention drives synchronization of alpha and beta rhythms between right inferior frontal and primary sensory neocortex. *Neuroscience,* 35(5), 2074–2082.

14 Traldi, L. 2016. Why do top managers prefer extreme sports? *Design@Large.* At http://www.designatlarge.it/why-top-managers-prefer-extreme-sports/?lang=en

15 Ward, M. 2017. Jeff Bezos and Bill Gates both do this mundane chore that may have significant mental benefits. CNBC, November 10. At https://www.cnbc.com/2017/11/10/why-jeff-bezos-and-bill-gates-both-do-this-mundane-chore.html

16 Traldi, L. 2016. Why do top managers prefer extreme sports? *Design@Large.* At http://www.designatlarge.it/why-top-managers-prefer-extreme-sports/?lang=en

17 Goudreau, J. 2015. 14 things successful people do before breakfast. *World Economic Forum.* At https://www.weforum.org/agenda/2015/11/14-things-successful-people-do-before-breakfast/

18 Eckfeldt, B. 2015. Why Ironmen and Ironwomen make great CEOs. *Forbes*. At https://www.forbes.com/sites/entrepreneursorganization/2015/07/14/why-ironmen-and-ironwomen-make-great-ceos/#35db92ed3e4d

19 Gailliot, M. and Baumeister, R. 2007. The physiology of willpower: Linking blood glucose to self-control. *Personality and Social Psychology Review*, 11(4), 303–327.

20 Diamond, A. 2013. Executive functions. *Annual Review of Psychology*, 64, 135–168.

21 Mischel, W., Shoda, Y. and Rodriguez, M. 1989. Delay of gratification in children. *Science*, 244, 933–938; Mischel, W. *The marshmallow test: Mastering self-control*. Boston, MA: Little, Brown Spark.

22 See Louie, K. and Glimcher, P. 2010. Separating value from choice: Delay discounting activity in the lateral intraparietal area. *Journal of Neuroscience*, 30(16), 5498–5507.

23 Metcalfe, J. and Mischel, W. 1999. A hot/cool system analysis of delay of gratification: Dynamics of willpower. *Psychological Review*, 106(1), 3–19.

24 Baumeister, R. and Al Ghamdi, N. 2014. Relevance of willpower dynamics, self-control, and ego depletion to flawed student decision making. *International Journal of Education and Social Science*, 1(3), page 149.

25 Nolen, J. 2018. Walter Mischel. *Encyclopedia Britannica*. At https://www.britannica.com/biography/Walter-Mischel

26 Frankl, V. 1946. *Man's search for meaning*. Boston, MA: Beacon Press.

27 Devoe, D. 2012. Viktor Frankl's Logotherapy: The search for purpose and meaning. *Inquiries Journal*, 4(7). At http://www.inquiriesjournal.com/articles/660/3/viktor-frankls-logotherapy-the-search-for-purpose-and-meaning

28 Smith, E. 2013. There's more to life than being happy. *The Atlantic*. At https://www.theatlantic.com/health/archive/2013/01/theres-more-to-life-than-being-happy/266805/

29 Frankl quoting Sigmund Freud in Frankl, V. 1946. *Man's search for meaning*. Boston, MA: Beacon Press.

30 Frankl, V. 1946. *Man's search for meaning*. Boston, MA: Beacon Press, page 86.

31 Frankl, V. 1946. *Man's search for meaning*. Boston, MA: Beacon Press, page 88.

32 Smith, E. 2013. There's more to life than being happy. *The Atlantic*. At https://www.theatlantic.com/health/archive/2013/01/theres-more-to-life-than-being-happy/266805/

33 Antonovsky, A. 1979. *Health, stress and coping*. San Francisco, CA: Jossey-Bass.

34 Manson, M. 2016. *The subtle art of not giving a fuck*. New York: HarperCollins, page 43.

35 Frankl, V. 1946. *Man's search for meaning*. Boston, MA: Beacon Press.

36 Kahneman, D. 2012. Five ways to understand happiness. *Market Leader*, Quarter 1, page 10.

37 Manson, M. 2016 *The subtle art of not giving a fuck*. New York: HarperCollins.

38 Onoda, H. 1999. *No surrender: My thirty-year war*. Annapolis, MD: US Naval Institute Press.

39 McFadden, R. 2014. Hiroo Onoda, soldier who hid in jungle for decades, dies at 91. *New York Times*. At https://www.nytimes.com/2014/01/18/world/asia/hiroo-onoda-imperial-japanese-army-officer-dies-at-91.html

40 Robbins, S. and Judge, T. 2018. *Essentials of organizational behavior*. London: Pearson.

41 Frankl, V. 1946. *Man's search for meaning*. Boston, MA: Beacon Press, page 127.

42 Bucker, R. 2018. Resilienz: Kann man Führungskräften seelische Widerstandskraft beibringen? *Edition F*. At https://editionf.com/resilienz-bedeutung-entwicklung

43 Bucker, R. 2018. Resilienz: Kann man Führungskräften seelische Widerstandskraft beibringen? *Edition F*. At https://editionf.com/resilienz-bedeutung-entwicklung

44 Paul Polman of Unilever in an interview with McKinsey's Adam Bird. 2009. *McKinsey conversations with global leaders: Paul Polman of Unilever*. At https://www.mckinsey.com/business-functions/strategy-and-corporate-finance/our-insights/mckinsey-conversations-with-global-leaders-paul-polman-of-unilever

CHAPTER EIGHT

About leading teams and making decisions in extreme conditions

SUBTEXT: Decide before it happens

In contrast to many other climbers I have always mountaineered in teams. Working in teams in which members push each other has always been salient on my expeditions. I chose partners who had a positive attitude and saw the possibilities, and I dropped the ones who only saw the roadblocks. Synergizing our different strengths and compensating each other's weaknesses helped us in many difficult situations and extreme conditions. When putting teams together I have always looked for individuals who can contribute different skills, experiences, and particular competencies, while at the same time they have a certain level of general base know how in mountaineering or in the main activity of our project. This has been most illustrative in the X7 project. In 2013 we decided with six experienced competitive ski touring athletes to climb the highest mountain of each of the seven countries located in the Alps, east to west in seven days by foot, skies, and bike. In short X7 or 7 days, 7 summits, 7 countries, 7 athletes. By starting each ascent from the valley floor we covered 18,000 vertical meters and 180km on the flat. Each athlete added something particular to the team's success – daredevil Eric Hjorleifson was always the first one on the downhill regardless of the steepness of the descent, Mario Scanu was like a machine in grooming the ascent, Javier Martin de Villa was always leading the climbs when it got really technical, and Schorsch Nicakes had an amazing sense of orientation.

But as much as there was diversity in our competencies and skill sets, there was a great deal of unity or homogeneity in our goals and commitments. Over the years I learnt that teams can only be efficient if all team members share the same goals and expectations. Climbing a mountain in a team cannot work out if one team member 'just wants to try it', another one wants to make it to the peak at all costs, and the third member of the group wants to make it to Camp 3. A great lesson has been my Broad Peak expedition with Basti in 2009. From the start we had different objectives, different motivations, and different levels of confidence in ourselves. At the time of the expedition Basti's grief over the deadly accident of his brother two years earlier caught up with him. He wasn't really focused. But there was little to no communication between us. We did not share our concerns and doubts. We wrongly assumed that everything was as usual, like during so many other successful tours we had done together in the past. Consequently we failed not only our attempt to climb Broad Peak summit, but the failure also damaged our friendship. The experience at Broad Peak in 2009 was an important learning curve in terms of realizing how critical it is for teams and their members to have their expectations and goals aligned and to be completely devoted to them.

The Broad Peak tour in 2009 also taught me to discuss and make decisions about these goals, our expectations, and any other details and eventualities of an expedition long before the start. Working together in teams in extreme conditions requires full transparency and openness with each other beforehand. Today I work out or anticipate with my team mates early on in the preparation process any type of critical situation or scenario that could happen during our tour. And we must agree on the decisions that go with these situations. In other words, we try to make decisions for situations before they are happening. This is particularly important for high altitude mountaineering. Making clear and rational decisions at 8000m can be very difficult. You are completely exhausted and your throat is too dried out to communicate; and if you could communicate, the low level of oxygen at that altitude makes it sometimes very tough to think straight. And even if you could communicate and think straight at 8000m, you would quickly freeze to death if you take the time in the bitter cold and in thin air to discuss the pros and cons of each alternative for the particular challenge you are facing in that moment.

This is why we agree on decisions such as time limits or time gates that we set for our group to ensure that we are not running out of time later on during our descent. We call up our gate time that we set as a group for a particular point of the ascent – and if we are behind in time we turn around. This requires an immense amount of discipline and commitment to the group's agreements. You have to able to bend your ego. Turning around with the summit a few meters away can be extremely frustrating and tempting to be ignored. Alternatively, as a group we might pre-decide in Basecamp that each of us follows his own strategy from a certain point onwards of the ascent. Even though this might sound like a paradox – climbing as a team and following pre-agreed team decisions and then switching at a certain point to individual decision making – such agreements are particularly critical in speed ascents. Having the freedom to continue to the summit if you still feel strong enough, and being able to pack it in if you feel you are slowing down the team. This requires a great sense of self responsibility for one's own actions so that their consequences do not harm the group. I had Nicolas Bonnet turning around in our speed ascent at Manalsu in 2007, and Michael Hasenknopf during our speed ascent at Peak Lenin in 2017. Both realized that they slowed down and jeopardized the summit ascent; or worse, that they would put their own lives at risk if they continued. Our first rule has always been that everyone is responsible for himself and his decisions, as outside help or rescue might just not be possible in the death zone. Today many climbing tourists forget this and expect their teams or mountain guides to bring them to the summit at all costs. Last year's refusal by a Pakistani climber to turn around on his ascent of Mount Everest cost his Sherpa all his fingers due to frost bite, and his future as a mountain guide.

The decisions we make prior to any tour are not only to survive live-threatening events. Extreme situations can also be the weeks and months sitting on top of each other in Basecamps. The bad weather and the waiting and condemnation to idleness can create strong tensions and pressures in the group. That is when the character and attitude of each team member really shines through. And that is why you want to have this full transparency and openness with each other before any expedition or project. Honest communication is really critical. Knowing exactly how each one in the team ticks; being able to drop out before it is too late; and being able to discuss and agree on decisions for all possible scenarios on and off the mountain. While the technical skills on the mountain are crucial, to function as a team you depend on each other's interpersonal skills and the personal relationships you have amongst the team members. When you already jump at each other off the mountain, chances are that you equally fail to function as a team on the mountain – and that can be deadly.

You have to be really careful in such pressured environments. It is critical in such conditions to have the occasional change of scene that break the monotony of a Basecamp or that could act as a valve to steam off any hot air. I always tried to meet and talk to members of other groups or to talk about topics that have nothing to do with climbing and mountaineering. The best remedy for me not to get stir crazy has always been the calls with my family back home. These calls with my kids and wife have been like ice cream is for a child.

Throughout the expedition or tour we usually have some formal leader or manager who has organized the project and who has the overall responsibility for the operations and organization. In most cases this was the leader of the expedition agency which organized the expedition including everything up to Basecamp. From Basecamp onwards we were on our own. The expedition leader was usually not part of the speed team. On the mountain my group usually works with situational leaders matching the situational demands with the strength of individual team members. In other words, if the task at hand is a technical climb then the best climber in our group takes the lead; if the task is a steep downhill ski descent then our best skier takes the lead. Considering the continuously changing conditions on a climb we work like a zipper with a continuous flow of leadership changes. This approach requires for everybody on the team to be aware that each one will have the responsibility for the group at some point. And on any mountain making a mistake as the leader could have very serious consequences for the whole team. When you are leading you usually choose the route which is the safest and the most efficient for your team. You groom the path and the others follow – often blindly because they are exhausted; because it is difficult to think straight; because they trust you. There must be mutual trust amongst all team members and a great sense of equality – otherwise this way of leading and following would not work out. The mutual trust in each other's competencies and strengths takes away much of the anxieties and fears that you encounter in extreme situations. It is often the sharing of fears and of the strenuous efforts that keep you going in the dark moments of climbing a mountain.

Photo 8.1 *With four friends at Piz Palü summit ridge 3850m (Swiss alps) during a four day speed rush through the Alps which we named X4. Standing for crossing the Alps from north to south all human powered. Starting in Germany climbing the highest summit Zugspitze (2962m); to Austria, summiting Mount Similaun (3603m); to Italy, Ortler (3905 m), and to Switzerland, Piz Palü. Four days, four countries, four summits - X4. In total 400km and 13,200 altitude meters.*

Photo 8.2 *Team preparing the way up crossing a huge crevasse in the ice fall of Manaslu (8163m) during the acclimatization phase.*

EXTREME EVENTS AND CONDITIONS

Within organization studies an extreme event has been defined as an ' occurrence that may result in an extensive and intolerable magnitude of physical, psychological, or material consequences […] to organization members'; extreme conditions or an extreme context are environments 'where one or more extreme events are occurring or are likely to occur'.[1] When applying this definition to business operations, then there are many companies where such extreme situations are commonplace. And there are numerous business cases in which decision making and the leading of teams take place in extreme conditions.[2]

These extreme events and conditions are often associated with action loaded and dramatic life and death scenarios such as military combat, emergency rooms, natural disasters, accidents, and terrorist attacks. Ben's experiences from Basecamp show another and rather different form of extreme event – yet with equally extensive and intolerable consequences predominantly at a psychological level. This type of situation shared and experienced by many other organizations and their members including, for example, military units and their soldiers: In their teams they are often crammed up for weeks and months in the narrowest of spaces such as tents and army barracks waiting for their marching orders or their next deployment. Boredom, idleness, monotony, and dreariness dominate life in their camps and lead to tensions and serious psychological pressures that strain the relationships between the soldiers.

So far, neither the action loaded nor the idling extreme cases have received any significant attention by scholars of organizations and management. Within the leadership field, 'leadership in extreme contexts may be one of the least researched areas,'[3] whereas decision making under extreme conditions has been predominantly discussed in specialized fields such as the military.[4] This constriction of scholarly works comes as a surprise considering that it is most of all extreme situations that require competent and strong leadership, efficient team work, and effective decision-making.[5] One of the reasons as to why there are so few scholarly works in these areas in extreme contexts might be that many extreme decision-making and leadership situations are based on rare cases such as the Fukushima Daiichi nuclear disaster or the Tenerife airplane collision. This makes it difficult to put forward recommendations that can be generalized across businesses and the different contexts in which they are operating.

Ben's experiences in extreme conditions are neither rare nor unique events. Ben and his teams have been confronted with extreme situations consistently throughout their projects and expeditions – similar to the daily emergency calls to which a fire department or an accident and emergency department responds.[6] Like these business units, Ben's experiences of making decisions and working in teams in extreme conditions show patterns of dynamics and processes that can be applied and tailored to the particular business contexts within which individuals and organizations are confronted with extreme events and conditions.

DIVERSE SKILLS AND COMMON GOALS

Ben repeatedly highlights and illustrates how the diverse skills and experiences amongst his climbing partners have been critical to the success and achievements of his teams' projects. Or as well-known organizational theorist Karl Weick argues 'the greater the repertoire of responses you have on your team, the more things you can do'.[7] Ben's experiences and Weick's argument have been confirmed by researchers within the field of work group diversity assuming an elaboration perspective. They suggest that heterogeneous teams possess a wider range of task-relevant knowledge, competencies, and experiences, all of which may help group members make more informed decisions. From this perspective, heterogeneity on teams leads to greater creativity with regard to problem-solving and decision-making processes and to better group performance than does homogeneity.[8] However, researchers employing a categorization perspective (in-group/out-group) argue that greater homogeneity within work groups leads to stronger group cohesion, greater member commitment, fewer interpersonal conflicts, and lower member turnover rates. These studies conclude that homogeneity leads to better group performance than does heterogeneity.[9]

While management scholars continue to be divided by taking either an elaboration or categorization perspective toward group diversity and group performance, Ben illustrates how group homogeneity and heterogeneity can be complementary and beneficial to the team. By creating and working in teams with diverse skill sets and experiences, and by simultaneously insisting on a strong commitment from all team members toward shared goals and expectations, he avails the acclaimed benefits of both perspectives – greater task-relevant knowledge and experiences to make more informed decisions and ensuring group cohesion and commitment to the group's shared goals. Higher group cohesiveness not only correlates with high group performance in normal situations[10]; teams with a strong sense of solidity and common goals also perform better in crises and extreme situations.[11] Group cohesion reduces stress and anxiety, and absorbs the fears group members have when facing extreme situations.[12] Reinhold Messner, the first mountaineer to solo climb Mount Everest without oxygen, explains this group phenomenon in a similar way:

> When alone you cannot share the fear…with a climbing buddy to be able to divide the fear into two parts leaves you with only half of the fear. When I first solo climbed the Nanga Parbat[13] I was filled with fear beyond belief. I just wanted to get down. I was too scared to be alone, to be only with myself up there on this mountain. I needed five years to learn to come to terms with my fears to be alone that high up on a mountain.[14]

ALIGNING EXPECTATIONS, MOTIVATIONS, AND OBJECTIVES

For Ben to ensure that individual expectations, motivations, and goals of his climbing partners are all aligned throughout the project, he conducts open and fully transparent discussions amongst all team members prior to every project. After his Broad Peak 2009 experience with Basti, Ben realized that regardless how well you know your teammates from previous expeditions, every subsequent project is different and every member's attitude and expectations might have changed since the last project. After two to three years teams 'can get too familiar and their effectiveness starts to decrease. The group members fall into a more routine patterns of interaction'. The teams break up and their members leave to find new challenges somewhere else.[15]

OPEN DISCUSSIONS PRIOR TO THE EVENT

Regardless whether it is about facing extreme weather conditions in 8000m altitude or a terrorist attack in a hotel[16] or government building[17] – the key to overcome successfully an extreme situation is foresight and preparedness.[18] While the extremity of a particular situation or context can motivate team members to engage intensely, they are often less effective in their actions. They are more likely to accept hasty decisions that may be poorly determined, inaccurate, and without clear direction. Without the preparedness for an extreme event the extremity can become too overwhelming, and individual team members become 'immobilized due to experiences of terror and other emotive responses to fear'.[19] Just like Ben learnt it the hard way in Peru and at Broad Peak, company leaders and their organizations need to accept that the 'it cannot happen to us' paradigm no longer withstands today's times of unpredictability and uncertainty.[20]

Team diversity can play an important role in challenging this paradigm by encouraging increased possibilistic thinking that is critical to better anticipate and foresee extreme events.[21] The anticipation also includes predicting potential tensions and interpersonal conflicts between team members that could intensify the event's extremity. Once identified, these potential personified trouble spots need to be discussed and eliminated before facing the extreme situation. When Michael Krzyzewski was asked in an interview what he would do in such a crisis situation, the three times Olympic winner as head coach of the US men's national basketball team simply explained that 'it's too late'.[22] It is about creating an environment where such conflicts do not happen in the first place.[23] Richard Marcinko, the founder of the highly acclaimed US Naval Special Warfare Unit Sea Air and Land (SEAL) Team Six used to take his team to a bar the night before deployment. There the alcohol ensured that any tensions between the soldiers surfaced eventually and would be dealt with by the soldiers in the bar before heading for their mission the next morning.[24] This is not to say that teams facing extreme situations or extreme conditions should get drunk together before they start their project. It is only to illustrate how teams in different organizational contexts realize the importance of transparent and open exchanges about individuals' motivations and expectations prior to their tasks at hand.

EGALITARIANISM AND TRUST WITHIN THE TEAM

In the business world teams and decision-making bodies are often sprinkled with strong egos and streaked by informal hierarchies or invisible power and seniority structures in which a few individuals dominate and influence the discussions and control for their outcomes. Peer pressure and group conformity are some of the means employed to suppress differing views and perspectives, and to force alignments and agreements.[25] Reaching genuine unanimity requires a sense of egalitarianism between the different team members and a blending of their egos. This is why, for example, in military special forces such as the British Special Air Service (SAS) units operate without the strict hierarchical rankings generally known in the military. All members are considered equal and often operate as self-managed teams in extreme conditions behind enemy lines. In the US SEAL team units waive standard dress codes and divisions between officers and lower ranks.[26]

Reaching genuine unanimity requires also mutual trust between the different team members. Trust in being able to share an opinion that differs from the majority view, trust that all viewpoints and suggestions are explored and incorporated in the final group goals and expectations. And the trust that whatever has been agreed prior of getting into the extreme situation will be upheld in the actual event. It is easy to agree on a 'no man left behind strategy' before hitting the battle field or fighting a wild-fire, yet it is a different matter to put one's own life at risk to save that of a comrade when being shot at, or when being surrounded by blazing trees and heavy smoke. Any hesitation or reservation of team members falls away 'only if they can trust that others will follow through on their commitments.'[27]

TASK ORIENTED LEADERSHIP ROTATION

A sense of egalitarianism, and trust in each other and in each other's skills and experiences is also critical when teams apply a situational leadership approach that Ben and his climbing partners use on their tours in extreme conditions. Depending on the challenge or task ahead, Ben's team changes its leader according to whoever in the team has the most relevant technical skills for the task. In extreme situations such a task oriented leadership approach is the most appropriate method. Self-managed teams operating in extreme conditions are more effective when they are led by leaders who rely on their expertise rather than any other forms of legitimate means of authority.[28] Often 'there is no time for talking things over and explaining decisions. Behavior must be automatic.'[29]

Within the military context in combat situations such a task oriented leadership rotation is considered dynamic subordination, 'where leadership is fluid and defined by conditions on the ground'. Or as a SEAL commander explains: 'the person who knows what to do next is the leader. We're entirely nonhierarchical in that way. When someone steps up to become the new leader, everyone, immediately, automatically, moves with him'.[30] In other words, when team members rotate as team leaders in extreme events, confidence in each other's competencies is absolute. Failure to trust the team member who leads can damage the team's cohesion and commitment.[31] In extreme situations such as extended periods of stress, teams whose members have faith in the team member who leads according to the task at hand, tend to be more effective and focused on their goals and objectives.[32] In extreme situations or contexts trust becomes a function of context and task instead of being 'only associated with specific individuals'.[33]

Sharing the leadership amongst team members allows for the team to sustain its performance in extreme events, as the rotation process allows for team members to recover while others lead, and for the incessant access to expertise and skills that is critical in an extreme context.[34] In civilian organizations that operate in extreme and highly risky environments this leadership rotation has been described by some scholars as team scaffolding that 'allows for extremely fluid groups of people to coordinate their work and increase the efficiency of the operations in a way that purely role based team work do not allow'.[35] Shift schedules and irregular working hours are illustrative examples of such fluidity. Other organizational scholars have coined the rotation of team leaders facing extreme events 'dynamic delegation' whereby the active leadership role is delegated to and withdrawn from team leaders by more senior leaders in response to the task demands.[36] In the presence of such hierarchical structures or seniority, and different levels of expertise, dynamic delegation 'not only addresses effectively the challenges of an extreme event, but it simultaneously increases managers and workers' skills and competencies thanks to the "deindividualized" team structures'.[37] These team structures are considered an 'investment of leadership in positions rather than individual people' that ensures that team members do not take offence when being superseded by another team member in leading the team.[38]

Such dynamic or fluid leadership rotation processes have been described as group flow and key to top group performances that are particularly required in extreme conditions. American psychologist Keith Sawyer, a former doctoral student of Mihaly Csikszentmihalyi,[39] studied group dynamics that lead to high group performances. He discovered that high performance groups attain a collective state of mind that he called group flow: 'Group flow is a peak experience, a group performing at its top level of ability. In group flow, […] the group acts without thinking about it first'.[40] Just like Ben explains, all decisions have been made beforehand; within the actual event all goes without saying, decisions and training routines are called up in the very situation. Within a business context such groups are also described as high energy teams 'in which ideas flow freely and its members build effortlessly on one another's work'. Members of such teams are considered energizers or persons 'who can spark progress on projects or within groups'.[41]

CREATING GROUP FLOW AND HIGH ENERGY TEAMS FACING EXTREME EVENTS

Creating such group flow or high energy in teams – critical in extreme events or under extreme conditions – requires the above discussed shared vision, mutual trust, the sense of egalitarianism and blend of egos, and the equal participation in the planning and execution of a project. The preparatory discussions and communications which are so critical prior to the extreme event require deep listening from all team members. Team members with preconceived ideas and plans can block new and innovative ways of how to address an extreme event or a situation in extreme conditions.[42] Allowing for ideas to flow without prejudices and biases encourages team members to focus on the possibilities rather than the constraints that 'keep ideas from ever getting off the ground'.[43]

As in Ben's case, the diversity of the team in terms of their particular knowledge and skills provides the necessary creative problem-solving skills and possibilistic thinking. 'If group members are too similar, flow becomes less likely – because the group interaction is no longer challenging [...] and nothing new and unexpected will ever emerge'.[44] High levels of shared general base know-how amongst team members can also increase problem-solving creativity. The shared expertise creates familiarity with the extreme challenge and context at hand.

The group has a common language, a shared knowledge base, and a communication style based on unspoken understandings.[45] This unspoken understanding or tacit knowledge ensures greater decision-making effectiveness and problem-solving creativity.[46]

Rotating leadership to ensure flow within the group requires complete concentration in the actual situation. In group flow the whole team focuses on the task, while 'other things are put out of mind. Small annoyances aren't noticed, and the external rewards that may or may not await at the end of the task are forgotten.'[47] What counts is the here and now. Regardless whether this is an 8000m summit, a battle field, or a boardroom – in contrast to general belief – facing extreme situations can happen to all of us.

KEY ARGUMENTS AND TAKEAWAYS:

- Challenge the 'it cannot happen to us' paradigm and encourage possibilistic thinking in open discussions prior to any project in extreme conditions. By doing so, you can better anticipate and foresee the challenges associated with extreme events and predict potential tensions and interpersonal conflicts between team members that could intensify an event's extremity.
- Encourage diversity of skills and competencies in your team. Greater range of task-relevant knowledge and experiences combined with increased possibilistic thinking help group members to make more informed decisions and have greater problem-solving creativity.
- Ensure high levels of shared general base know-how within the team to create familiarity with the extreme challenge and context at hand. The unspoken understanding or tacit knowledge ensures greater decision-making effectiveness and problem-solving creativity amongst team members.

(Continued)

- Create a shared vision and ensure the commitment from all team members toward shared goals and expectations prior to a project in extreme conditions. Teams with strong group cohesion and a strong sense of solidity perform better in crises and extreme situations.
- Create a sense of egalitarianism and blend egos in your teams before being confronted with extreme contexts or extreme events. By doing so you support a genuine unanimity amongst team members and their shared goals and expectations.
- Ensure mutual trust between all team members. This trust is critical in extreme situations when team members rely on each other's integrity between their words and actions and on following through on their commitments.
- Insist on deep listening by all team members in every discussion. This ensures that team members avoid preconceived ideas and plans that can block new and innovative ways of how to address an extreme event or a situation in extreme conditions.
- Rotate leadership to match the technical skills of the leader with the challenges the group faces. This task oriented leadership approach ensures greater concentration in the extreme event, and sustains the team's performance as the rotation process allows for team members to recover while others lead.

NOTES

1 Hannah, S., Uhl-Bien, M. Avolio, B. and Cavarretta, F. 2009. A framework for examining leadership in extreme contexts. *The Leadership Quarterly*, 20, page 898.
2 Hannah, S., Uhl-Bien, M. Avolio, B. and Cavarretta, F. 2009. A framework for examining leadership in extreme contexts. *The Leadership Quarterly*, 20, 897–919.

3 Hannah, S., Uhl-Bien, M. Avolio, B. and Cavarretta, F. 2009. A framework for examining leadership in extreme contexts. *The Leadership Quarterly*, 20, page 897.

4 March, J. and Weissinger-Baylon, R. 1986. *Ambiguity and command*. New York: Longman Inc.

5 See Gal, R. and Jones, F. 1985. Psychological aspects of combat stress: A model derived from Israeli and other combat experiences. Unpublished manuscript; Dynes, R., Quarantelli, E. and Kreps, G. 1981. *A perspective on disaster planning*. Newark, DE: Disaster Research Center, University of Delaware.

6 Hannah, S., Uhl-Bien, M. Avolio, B. and Cavarretta, F. 2009. A framework for examining leadership in extreme contexts. *The Leadership Quarterly*, 20, page 914.

7 A conversation between Diane Coutu and Karl Weick. 2003. Sense and reliability. *Harvard Business Review*, April, 83–90 (page 87).

8 See Carter, D., Simkins, B. and Simpson, W. 2003. Corporate governance, board diversity, and firm value. *The Financial Review*, 38, 33–53; Arfken, D., Bellar, S. and Helms, M. 2004. The ultimate glass ceiling revisited: The presence of women on corporate boards. *Journal of Business Ethics*, 50, 177–186.

9 See Jehn, K., Northcraft, G. and Neale, M. 1999. Why differences make a difference: A field study of diversity, conflict, and performance in workgroups. *Administrative Science Quarterly*, 44, 741–763; Simons, T., Pelled, L. and Smith, K. 1999. Making use of difference: Diversity, debate, and decision comprehensiveness in top management teams. *Academy of Management Journal*, 42, 662–674.

10 Sawyer, K. 2015. Group flow and group genius. *The North American Montessori Teachers' Association Journal*, 40(3), 29–52.

11 Wright, D. 1946. Anxiety in aerial combat. *Research Publication of the Association of Nervous and Mental Disorders*, 25, 116–124.

12 Strachan, E., Schimel, J., Arndt, J., Williams, T., Solomon, S., Pyszczynski, T., et al. (2007). Terror mismanagement evidence that mortality salience exacerbates phobic and compulsive behaviors. *Personality and Social Psychology Bulletin*, 33, 1137–1151.

13 Ninth highest mountain in the world at 8126m above sea level.

14 Televised interview with Markus Lanz on October 17, 2013. At https://www.youtube.com/watch?v=pTSzw4xac14

15 Sawyer K. 2015. Group flow and group genius. *The North American Montessori Teachers' Association Journal*, 40(3), pages 41–42.

16 The 2008 terrorist attacks in South Mumbai at the Oberoi Trident Hotel and the Taj Palace & Tower.

17 The 9/11 terrorist attacks against the Pentagon.

18 McConnell, A. and Drennan, L. (2006). Mission impossible? Planning and preparing for crisis. *Journal of Contingencies and Crisis Management*, 14, 59–70.

19 Hannah, S., Uhl-Bien, M. Avolio, B. and Cavarretta, F. 2009. A framework for examining leadership in extreme contexts. *The Leadership Quarterly*, 20, page 903.

20 Foldy, E., Goldman, L. and Ospina, S. 2008. Sensegiving and the role of cognitive shifts in the work of leadership. *The Leadership Quarterly*, 19, 514–529.

21 Clarke, L. 2006. *Worst cases: Terror and catastrophe in the popular imagination*. Chicago, IL: University of Chicago Press

22 Interview with Michael Krzyzewski. At https://www.youtube.com/watch?v=Phny1h4AZ0Y

23 Krzyzewski, M. and Phillips, D. 2000. *Leading with the heart*. New York: Warner Books.

24 Marcinko, R. 1992. *Rogue warrior*. New York: Pocket Books.

25 See Asch, S. 1951. Effects of group pressure upon the modification and distortion of judgment. In H. Guetzkow (Ed.) *Groups, leadership and men*. Pittsburgh, PA: Carnegie Press.

26 Kotler, S. and Wheal, J. 2017. *Stealing fire*. New York: HarperCollins.

27 Cross, R., Baker, W. and Parker, A. 2003. What creates energy in organization? *MIT Sloan Management Review*, Summer, page 56.

28 Druskat, V. and Wheeler, J. 2003. Managing from the boundary: The effective leadership of self-managing work teams. *Academy of Management Journal*, 46, 435–457.

29 Hersey P. and Blanchard, K. 1996. Great ideas revisited: Revisiting the life-cycle theory of leadership. *Training and Development*, 50(1), page 45.

30 Kotler, S. and Wheal, J. 2017. *Stealing fire*. New York: HarperCollins, page 14.

31 Hamby, J. 2002. The mutiny wagon wheel: A leadership model for mutiny in combat. *Armed Forces & Society*, 28, 575–600.

32 Sweeney, P., Thompson, V. and Blanton, H. 2009. Trust and influence in combat: An interdependence model. *Journal of Applied Social Psychology*, 39, 235–264.

33 Hällgren, M., Rouleau, L. and De Rond, M. 2018. A matter of life or death: How extreme context research matters for management and organization studies. *Academy of Management Annals*, 12(1), page 120.

34 Valentine, M. and Edmondson, A. 2015. Team scaffolds: How mesolevel structures enable role-based coordination in temporary groups. *Organization Science*, 26(2), 405–422.

35 Hällgren, M., Rouleau, L. and De Rond, M. 2018. A matter of life or death: How extreme context research matters for management and organization studies. *Academy of Management Annals*, 12(1), page 120.

36 Klein, K., Ziegert, J., Knight, A. and Xiao, Y. 2006. Dynamic delegation: Shared, hierarchical, and deindividualized leadership in extreme action teams. *Administrative Science Quarterly*, 51(4), 590–621.

37 Hällgren, M., Rouleau, L. and De Rond, M. 2018. A matter of life or death: How extreme context research matters for management and organization studies. *Academy of Management Annals*, 12(1), page 120.

38 Klein, K., Ziegert, J., Knight, A. and Xiao, Y. 2006. Dynamic delegation: Shared, hierarchical, and deindividualized leadership in extreme action teams. *Administrative Science Quarterly*, 51(4), page 616.

39 Mihaly Csikszentmihalyi coined the term flow in Csikszentmihalyi, M. 1990. *Flow: The psychology of optimal experience*. New York: HarperCollins Publishers.

40 Sawyer, K. 2015. Group flow and group genius. *The North American Montessori Teachers' Association Journal*, 40(3), page 33.

41 Cross, R., Baker, W. and Parker, A. 2003. What creates energy in organization? *MIT Sloan Management Review*, Summer, 51–56.

42 See Sawyer, K. 2015. Group flow and group genius. *The North American Montessori Teachers' Association Journal*, 40(3), 29–52.

43 Cross, R., Baker, W. and Parker, A. 2003. What creates energy in organization? *MIT Sloan Management Review*, Summer, page 56.

44 Sawyer, K. 2015. Group flow and group genius. *The North American Montessori Teachers' Association Journal*, 40(3), page 38.

45 Kotler, S. and Wheal, J. 2017. *Stealing fire*. New York: HarperCollins, page 133.

46 Sawyer, K. 2015. Group flow and group genius. *The North American Montessori Teachers' Association Journal*, 40(3), 29–52.

47 Sawyer, K. 2015. Group flow and group genius. *The North American Montessori Teachers' Association Journal*, 40(3), 37.

CHAPTER NINE

About speed and lightness

SUBTEXT: Slow down to be fast

Speed and lightness are the key attributes that have accompanied me my whole life. When I started in competitive cross-country skiing it was always about speed and about winning competitions. Lightness was less of an issue – we never carried much with us on competitions. From cross-country skiing, I slowly moved to ski mountaineering. Within the mountaineering scene most people I met had a traditional mountaineering background. And within this environment having the right equipment was essential. And by right I mean being functional and as light as possible. My climbing buddies and I became obsessed by this notion of lightness – in particular as I realized that in mountaineering speed largely depends on this lightness factor. Much of what I knew about material lightness came from my time in the ski touring national team between 2003–2006. Within the mountaineering context, the goal was to transfer this expertise to speed mountaineering the highest peaks of the world.

This is why we focused on our body weight and what goes into our backpacks. In terms of our body weight we had no problems losing in our intensive training sessions some of the kilos we gained with the few too many beers we had in the off season. When it comes to what goes into the backpack, this was an entirely different story. It was more difficult to decide what we did not take, than what we needed to take. We had to decide what was really essential and what could be left at Basecamp. And to agree on the essentials was difficult. Apart from Hans Kammerlander, few have ever considered speed mountaineering as a formal approach. We entered a completely new terrain here. What we knew was that every gram too much could slow us down and prevent us from making it to the top within our agreed time window.

Of course we could not drill holes in our ski boots like we used to do in ski mountaineering competitions. But we cut off half of the shoelaces of our running shoes, we cut parts off the plastic shafts of our ski boots, and we trimmed clothing down to the minimum. We discussed whether we needed 1.7l or 1.8l of water; everything was measured down to the bare essentials. And everything was calculated in relation to our time budget. The time we would allow ourselves to make it to the top and back down again. Within this time frame we discussed and agreed when and what we would eat, and when and how much we would drink. In this way we were able to count how many gels and how much water we needed. And in this way we ended up with our 12kg backpack that we carried from Basecamp to the summit. The whole decision-making process of what are the essentials and what can be dropped and omitted was not just time consuming and complex; to get it right we had to be rigid and thorough in our reasoning.

The process was also a learning experience in terms of simplifying a complex task to its key essentials. The physical lightness of our equipment needed to be combined with the optimization of the procedures during the climb. We had to perfect our actions and movements. Every move had to be optimized in terms of using the least amount of energy and being as fast as possible. My climbing partner Schorsch developed a tool that allowed us to take off our ski skins without having to open our ski bindings. We developed external ski carrier systems on our backpacks which allowed us to get to our skies without having to drop the bags, and without having to open and close them. We developed a ski shoe with only one buckle instead of the traditional four buckles, and an extra activation mechanism for the ski/walk system. This one buckle did not only close or open the boot, but also closed or opened the movement of the cuff at the same time allowing us to switch from walk into ski mode and vice versa. And while we were at it, we developed pants with an opening for this buckle so that we did not have to pull up our pants and gators like we had to do in the past with the four buckles. This novel combination of one buckle and its pants' opening reduced our hand movements from six to only one. Much of the optimization was about simplifying the handlings and reducing our movements to a minimum. But optimization also meant developing motion sequences that kept a natural flow instead of relying on disruptive or abnormal movements. For example, as we could not use big mittens to work our equipment and clothes, we invented mittens with a hole on the side of the palm. Inside the mittens we would have thinner finger gloves which I could just move through the hole to handle any more delicate jobs without taking off the mittens. By creating and applying all these novelties, we saved ourselves time and energy.

The undisrupted flow of our movements helped us to keep a rhythm. This pushed us into a flow state. Everything was flowing. Our movements were smooth, without disruption, and reduced to a minimum. We felt we were on the right track, and we had made the right decisions beforehand. The flow made us euphoric and confident. And it is this sense of euphoria and the self-confidence that often lead to the misguided temptation to move faster. Over the years I learnt that a steady rhythm is much more effective than starting too fast or too slow. Most often we are tempted to start a race or an activity at full speed, or at least way too fast without taking regularly the time to eat or drink – only to be exhausted long before the finish line or the end of the activity. But knowing your right speed and having breaks requires a great self-awareness, self-knowledge, and self-control. Without this self-consciousness, climbing too fast or too slow in the death zone can mean certain serious health risks and death. For my climbing partners and me speed was therefore not a question of kilometres or meters per hour, but rhythm, fluency, and steadiness.

With my experiences from training and experimenting in lower altitudes I felt more comfortable and confident to ascend an 8000m summit using a speed style with minimum weight and the right rhythm than with the traditional mountaineering method which included different stages and camps at different altitudes. In a speed ascent we spend only few hours in the death zone versus other climbers who could stay for several days above 6000m to move slowly camp by camp to the summit. In contrast to these mountaineers we need only a small good weather window of 18–24 hours. And we spend relatively little time in an extremely low oxygen environment. The latter causes headaches, nausea, and a speedy loss of energy, and prevents you from recovering or recharging your batteries.

In particular the loss of energy can be critical when it comes to making it back down. When you are climbing in these altitudes your body burns an immense amount of energy in a very short time. Even when these traditional climbers are only sleeping or resting, at 7000m, these activities reduce your energy storages rapidly. It is very difficult to replace this energy by eating enough energy gels or other forms of energy. In fact you feel so exhausted that you find it difficult to eat at all; your throat is swollen and hurts, your mouth and lips are frozen and you hardly feel anything, and every bite can cost more energy than you eat. Thus, statistically, most mountaineers die of exhaustion on their way back, after having used all their energy storages during their ascent to the summit.

With these points in mind, it becomes clear that it is not the speed in the traditional sense that makes me faster. The interplay of lightness, movement at a steady rhythm, and the limited time in the death zone on my way up allow me to save energy for my way back down to Basecamp. This brings up the question why not everybody uses the speed mountaineering approach. For one, there is the physical and mental fitness aspect. There is still a difference between ascending in one go from Basecamp to the summit without oxygen and without porters versus ascending with oxygen and porters step by step. Some observers have criticized rightly the fact that almost anybody with enough money can make it up Mount Everest. Sherpas prepare the tracks, carry food, tents, extra oxygen tanks, and all the other equipment from camp to camp, set up each camp and cook for the expedition members. The latter work their way upwards with the help of oxygen and their personal Sherpas by their side. Another reason is of course that not everybody is capable of, or dares to ski down from an 8000m peak. Then, with the strict time line and carrying the bare essentials, there is little to no space for any errors or unexpected eventualities that could delay the ascent. There is no room for any trial and error. Not everybody can and wants to invest the time and energy in the extensive preparation to minimize the uncertainties that come with the mountaineering of an 8000m mountain.

If something unanticipated did happen, however, I would have to act rapidly and often make quick decisions. The speed with which you take your decisions in those low oxygen environments and icy weather conditions can save your life. In those situations the lightness could be somewhat the cause for being in trouble and having to make fast decisions. For example, when you are hit by an unexpected whiteout or snow storm, and you have no tent or sleeping bag to set up an emergency bivouac. Yet as this lightness comes with a clear set of procedures and routines, it can also act as a factor that enables fast decisions. When you hit your planned time limit 50 altitude meters below the summit, the decision is that you turn around, without any second thoughts or discussions.

These fast decisions enabled by the lightness are only possible because the preparation includes worst case scenarios, possible eventualities and scenarios, and contingency plans. And of course making fast decisions requires discipline. Discipline to stick to the routines and decisions made prior to a situation that requires a decision. Preparation and self-control have helped me to keep calm in precarious situations. Panicking or being hectic and stressed will only make you lose vital energy on a mountain.

Speed in speed mountaineering and speed climbing has a different meaning from speed in car racing or other racing activities. Surviving in high altitude and making it back to Basecamp fast, means going slow and steady. It means patience. Taking your time in the preparation and realizing that one cannot move from cross-country skiing to ascending an 8000m peak. Taking your time in acclimatizing your body to the higher altitude, and not risking an early ascend only because the weather is right. And taking your time in training your body to find the rhythm that gets you into that crucial energy-saving flow mode. All this can take years, with ups and downs, with successes and failures. And in all of this, lightness plays an important role – lightness to accept the failures and to put them into perspective; lightness to turn around when you still have enough time and energy to make it back safely; and the lightness to keep the dreams alive that you have had since a kid wanting to conquer all the mountains around you.

Photo 9.1 *Ben fully concentrated skiing down the steep slopes of Broad Peak (8051m) in no fall terrain.*

Photo 9.2 *Ben on the way to Camp 1 at Shisha Pangma (8027m).*

Like with so many other interrelated and interdependent concepts discussed in this book, this chapter's lightness and speed also go hand in hand. Speed in the mountaineering sense allows Ben to be lighter while his lightness makes him faster. And as has been the case for many of the themes that we have addressed throughout this book, there are only few management and organization studies, texts, or concepts which have addressed lightness and speed in the conventional sense or in the way described by Ben in the context of mountaineering.

LIGHTNESS

LIGHTNESS AS A PHYSICAL CONCEPT AT AN ORGANIZATIONAL LEVEL

At an organizational level the management concept that comes closest to Ben's idea of lightness from an operational perspective or in a material sense is the notion of lean management. Lean management has emerged as a response to the economic downturn at the beginning of the twenty-first century and the urgent need for companies to save costs and to be more receptive to customer demands.[1] The concept originated in Japan after World War II. Car manufacturing companies such as Toyota were forced by the destruction of the country's infrastructure and facilities to produce their cars with 'lesser inventory, human effort, investment, and defects'.[2] Toyota's approach was considered lean because it used less, or the minimum, of everything required to produce a product or perform a service.[3] Lean management has been associated with concepts such as 'Just in Time'[4] and 'Total Quality Management'[5] and has focused predominantly on manufacturing industries and their production and supply chain processes. Key objectives of lean management have been the continuous reduction and elimination of waste while maintaining or increasing the quality of products.[6]

Although numerous observers have praised the benefits of lean management, the concept can have negative implications in product design and development. By focusing only on the essentials and on speed in the traditional sense, a lean management approach can lead to 'products without markets' and without a 'story around the narrative of use'.[7] Minimization needs to be balanced with thoughtfulness of 'how a person experiences a given product in the context of the rest of their life'.[8] And just like Ben has highlighted how speed in the mountains is about patience and taking time for preparation, product design and development are also processes that take longer. They are about creating emotions around products – 'products that people love, not just products that people use'.[9] Lightness as a physical concept within an organizational context goes hand in hand with speed in Ben's mountaineering sense.

LIGHTNESS AS AN ORGANIZATIONAL STATE OF MIND

However, Ben's lightness within an organizational context goes beyond processes of material reductionism and operational lightness. His idea of lightness could also be described or considered as an organizational state of mind; an organizational mind-set that allows for companies to show greater flexibility, to be patient or to act fast, to make unconventional decisions, and to go nonconforming ways. These traits and an organizational lightness of the mind can often be observed in start-ups; when nascent firms' experimenting, daring and nonconforming ways of doing business are still not fully controlled and supressed by shareholders' pressures, other stakeholders' expectations, and by growing structural and procedural complexities. Once these pressures and measures are well established and set in place, organizational lightness is often replaced by an organizational cumbersomeness that slows down vital organizational changes and learning.

Or as Starbucks' Howard D. Schultz put it at a shareholders' meeting in 2010, 'we somehow evolved from a culture of entrepreneurship, creativity and innovation to a culture of, in a way, mediocrity and bureaucracy'.[10] As a result, Schultz introduced numerous strategic decisions and operational actions that have been described as Starbucks going back to its roots – providing an authentic coffeehouse experience and making great coffee. By doing so, Schultz restored Starbucks' organizational lightness – so important for a 'striking turnaround in the speed and spirit of innovation at Starbucks'.[11] Many companies today continue to experience a 'bureaucratic sclerosis'[12] similar to that of Starbucks prior to 2010, destroying their organizational lightness and sapping 'their organizations of creativity, willingness to take risk, and productivity'.[13] Few companies have made the necessary changes in form of returning to their core businesses, to what matters most to them, to what they are great at, and of cutting down on organizational structures and processes that have bottled-up their original organizational free spirit and lightness.

LIGHTNESS AS A MENTAL STATE

Behind the success or failure of companies to restore and sustain organizational lightness are their leaders and decision makers. In their day to day work-lives these executives and managers have been facing rapidly changing environments, increasingly complex challenges, and growing pressures from a wide range of stakeholders. Managers are often distracted by everyday activities and lose sight of what matters most to them and their organizations. These dynamics can take away an individual's mental lightness that is crucial to initiate the organizational changes that ensure the renewal or sustainability of organizational lightness.[14] This opposing interdependency of individual mental lightness and organizational complexity and cumbersomeness creates a downward spiral that can often be observed in nascent firms transforming into large businesses. At the start, company founders are often successful because they dare and take risks. They go in new and nonconforming ways. They succeed because they have a certain mental lightness and free spirit. With their success comes company expansion and growth. And this growth is usually managed with a standard formula in form of additional layers of managers bureaucratizing company structures and processes that can crush individuals' mental lightness.

Some entrepreneurs and their growing companies have addressed this phenomenon successfully. When Google's board decided that the company was growing too big for its founding fathers Larry Page and Sergey Brin, the two co-founders insisted on a CEO who could 'discipline Google's flamboyant, self-indulgent culture, without wringing out the genius'.[15] They recruited Eric Schmidt. Schmidt was not only an experienced software engineer but also an experienced Burning Man participant. And the latter experience was the decisive factor for Page and Brin. The annual Burning Man event in Nevada is about 'why not', free spirits searching for 'experiences beyond the pale of mainstream society'.[16] Page and Brin's unusual selection criteria paid off. During his reign at Google, Schmidt increased company revenues by 40,000 percent.[17] Google's focus on sustaining a state of lightness amongst all its ranks and files led to the introduction of its mindfulness center. In this center

Google offers meditation courses and means to help employees to relax and slow down.[18]

LIGHTNESS AS A PHYSICAL CONCEPT AT AN INDIVIDUAL LEVEL

Although meditation and other related mental exercises are well known for psychological benefits such as mental lightness, Ben illustrates through his experiences how mental lightness can also be achieved through physical lightness – the stripping down of one's material goods and belongings. The freeing of individuals from non-essentials that are slowing them down in their day to day activities at the workplace, their professional careers, and personal development has been explored by proponents of minimalism.

Minimalism has its roots in various art forms such as the visual arts, architecture, music, literature, design, and philosophies such as Zen Buddhism and its principles of austerity and simplicity.[19] Across these artistries and belief systems minimalism has been defined as stripped to the essentials. Minimalism along this line explored within a business or managerial context in management and organization studies is non-existent. The concept has been limited to a popular cultural artefact advocated by alternative lifestyle followers because it is opposed to what a traditional business approach promotes: buying more products more frequently. Yet, whether it is a growing sustainable consciousness or a search for meaning in life, more and more people have started to discover the benefits of having less:

> With less, it became easier to think, make decisions, and focus. I could cut through complex themes with ease. And the uncluttered closet led to less time deciding what to wear. My mind became unfettered. And my soul felt free. This shift in my approach allowed room to think. And space to sort.[20]

This CEO's experience illustrates how physical lightness can create a shift from *having* to *doing* and ultimately *becoming*. How physical lightness of *having* less leads to a mental state that *is* one of lightness.

SPEED

SPEED AS IN FAST

Ben and the above quoted CEO's experiences also show how their states of lightness allows them to make decisions easier and faster. This is not because they consider lightness as superficiality or light-heartedness, but because their physical lightness makes them have less while their mental lightness makes them need less. With less to focus on what one has and what one needs, one starts to see the bare essentials and what really matters. When one knows what matters and what is important, thinking becomes less distracted, one focuses on the task at hand and potentially enters a state of flow; decisions come effortless and faster.[21]

Speed and the notion of time have played an important role in the management discourse about thinking and decision-making processes. Nobel laureate in economics and senior scholar Daniel Kahneman's *Thinking, Fast and Slow*[22] is a comprehensive oeuvre that goes into great detail about the systems that influence our thinking, their workings, and mutual influences. Kahneman differentiates between System 1 and 2. System 1 produces fast and effortless thinking, and includes expert intuition, heuristic intuitive thoughts, 'as well as entirely automatic mental activities of perception and memory'.[23] System 2 is responsible for slow, effortful, and deliberate thinking. It is controlling thoughts and behaviors. When one is cognitively busy or overloaded by dealing with a variety of things at the same time, self-control is weakened, System 2 becomes overworked in regaining control and focus, energy levels deplete, and making decisions is cumbersome and will take longer. This is why Ben seeks so often a state of flow and mental lightness for which System 1 is responsible. In this state the focus is reduced to a particular task, 'maintaining this focused attention requires no exertion of self-control', energy can be freed and directed back to the task at hand, and decisions are made not only effortless but also faster.[24] Mental lightness creates speed in thinking and decision making.

SPEED AS IN SLOW AND PATIENT

But though decision speed has been recognized as a critical factor of individual and firm performance,[25] as the next competitive advantage[26] and secret weapon of all businesses,[27] Ben's experiences show how speed can also be defined differently from rapidity. On numerous occasions Ben demonstrated how slowing down and being patient helped him to become faster. The Zen story *The taste of Banzo's sword* is a timeless illustration of Ben's opposing interpretation and use of speed in the conventional sense:

> Matajuro Yagyu was the son of a famous swordsman. His father, believing that his son's work was too mediocre to anticipate mastership, disowned him. So Matajuro went to Mount Futara and there found the famous swordsman Banzo. But Banzo confirmed the father's judgment. "You wish to learn swordsmanship under my guidance?" asked Banzo. "You cannot fulfill the requirements." "But if I work hard, how many years will it take to become a master?" persisted the youth. "The rest of your life," replied Banzo. "I cannot wait that long," explained Matajuro. "I am willing to pass through any hardship if only you will teach me. If I become your devoted servant, how long might it be?" "Oh, maybe ten years," Banzo relented. "My father is getting old, and soon I must take care of him," continued Matajuro. "If I work far more intensively, how long would it take me?" "Oh, maybe thirty years," said Banzo. "Why is that?" asked Matajuro. "First you say ten and now thirty years. I will undergo any hardship to master this art in the shortest time!" "Well," said Banzo, "in that case you will have to remain with me for seventy years. A man in such a hurry as you are to get results seldom learns quickly".[28]

For Yagyu and any extreme athlete it takes time to make it to the top. It takes time to prepare and train; it takes time to have regular breaks to recover; and it takes time to be patient and wait for the right moment. In previous chapters we have described how athletes such as Alex Honnold, Reinhold Messner, Felix Baumgartner, and Gerlinde Kaltenbrunner prepared and waited years for their key moment or ultimate experience.

And it has not only been these athletes who have discovered slowness for their success, Napoleon Bonaparte had already recognized the advantages of slowness when he ordered to 'dress me slowly for I am in a hurry'.[29] And, more recently, business scholars and consultants have put forward arguments and evidence for why companies and managers might also want to consider slowing down.

In a study of 343 businesses, those which slowed down and paused at the right moment outperformed those which were permanently in a fast-paced state and focused on maximizing efficiency. The companies which slowed down 'improved their top and bottom lines, averaging 40 percent higher sales and 52 percent higher operating profits over a three year period'.[30] These higher performing companies understood that operational speed and strategic speed are two very different concepts. They took their time for strategic alignment, and to engage in more discussions, share ideas, encourage innovative thinking, and allow 'time to reflect and learn'.[31] Pauses for reflection and learning are particular important to companies that are growing. Uber's failure in South East Asia is just one example of how companies expanding and growing fast fail to build in strategic pauses in their growth strategy. If companies and their top teams slow down, 'they eventually go deeper and faster into achieving their objectives. They deal more effectively with increased complexity and challenges – and they use less energy'.[32] Taking time out for reflections and discussions at the right moment can lead to more collaborative and informed decisions. And what little time companies and their top teams lose in their decision-making process, they gain back in execution.

However, companies, business leaders, decision makers, and people in general are still far from accepting that slowing down or having regular breaks for reflection and taking a breath can be an effective alternative to our fast-paced lives. Instead we continue to believe that living at high speed is the secret to progress and prosperity. We eat fast food, have fast sex, read one-minute bed time stories to our kids, speed dial, speed read, speed walk, speed date, and speed yoga. We believe that pausing means falling behind, that stopping means failing. Ben's speed mountaineering experiences illustrate how being fast and making it to the top and back is about knowing when to slow down, when to turn around, and when to be patient. And Ben shows us how mental lightness provides the self-confidence and courage to overcome the fears and doubts of slowing down.

KEY ARGUMENTS AND TAKEAWAYS:

- Ensure you keep focused on what matters most to your business and at what your company is great. Challenge standardized, bureaucratizing structures and processes which lead to unnecessary organizational complexity and cumbersomeness. Prevent your organization and your employees from having their lightness being bottled up or crushed. Organizational and individual lightness are critical to your company's creativity and innovation, willingness to take risks, and ability to adapt to a rapidly changing and increasingly complex environment.
- Understand that operational speed and strategic speed are two very different concepts. Have your business and top teams take the occasional breather and take time out for strategic alignment, and to engage in more discussions, share ideas, encourage innovative thinking, and allow time to reflect and learn. Slowing down will help them to make better decisions and achieve their objectives faster. They will deal more effectively with increased complexity and challenges – and they use less energy.
- Understand what matters and is essential in your life. With this is mind consider having less of the nonessentials. Freeing yourself from *having* can help you to *becoming* lighter – physically and mentally. Lightness helps you to be faster – in your thinking and making decisions. Lightness also gives you the confidence to slow down, to turn around, to stop, and to be patient.

NOTES

1 Womack, J., Jones, D. and Roos, D. 1990. *The Machine that changed the world.* New York: Rawson Associates.

2 Bhamu, J. and Sangwan, K. 2014. Lean manufacturing: Literature review and research issues. *International Journal of Operations and Production Management*, 34(7), page 876.

3 Bhamu and Sangwan in reference to Hayes, R. and Pisano, G. 1994. Beyond world-class – the new manufacturing strategy. *Harvard Business Review*, 72(1), 77–76.

4 Monden, Y. 1983. *The Toyota production system.* Portland, OR: Productivity Press.

5 Basu, R. 2001, Six sigma to fit sigma: The third wave of operational excellence. *Institution of Industrial Engineers Solutions*, June, 28–33.

6 Womack, J. and Jones, D. 1996. *Lean thinking.* New York: Simon & Schuster; Holloway, L. and Hall, A. 1997. Principle of lean management. *Industry and Higher Education*, 11(4), 241–245.

7 Kolko, J. 2015. Lean doesn't always create the best products. *Harvard Business Review*, May 14. At https://hbr.org/2015/05/lean-doesnt-always-create-the-best-products, page 3–4.

8 Kolko, J. 2015. Lean doesn't always create the best products. *Harvard Business Review*, May 14. At https://hbr.org/2015/05/lean-doesnt-always-create-the-best-products, page 4.

9 Kolko, J. 2015. Lean doesn't always create the best products. *Harvard Business Review*, May 14. At https://hbr.org/2015/05/lean-doesnt-always-create-the-best-products, page 5.

10 Stone, B. 2008. Starbucks plans to return to its roots. *New York Times*, March 20. At https://www.nytimes.com/2008/03/20/business/20sbux.html

11 Stone, B. 2008. Starbucks plans to return to its roots. *New York Times*, March 20. At https://www.nytimes.com/2008/03/20/business/20sbux.html

12 Hamel, G. and Zanini, M. 2017. What we learned about bureaucracy from 7000 HBR readers. *Harvard Business Review*, August 10. At https://hbr.org/2017/08/what-we-learned-about-bureaucracy-from-7000-hbr-readers?utm_medium=email&utm_source=newsletter_daily&utm_campaign=dailyalert&referral=00563&spMailingID=17853288&spUserID=MTM5NjExMzY1MTQzS0&spJobID=1080656592&spReportId=MTA4MDY1NjU5MgS2

13 Hamel, G. and Zanini, M. 2018. The end of bureaucracy. *Harvard Business Review*, November–December, 51–59.

14 Gunn, B. 2001. The incredible lightness of being focused. *Strategic Finance*, 82(11), 12–15.

15 John Markoff of the *New York Times* quoted by Kotler, S. and Wheal, J. 2017. *Stealing fire*. New York: HarperCollins; Kotler, S. 2014. *The rise of superman*. New York: HarperCollins, page 18.

16 The Attic. 2018. *How Burning Man got so hot*. At https://www.theattic.space/home-page-blogs/2018/8/16/how-burning-man-got-so-hot

17 Kotler, S. and Wheal, J. 2017. *Stealing fire*. New York: HarperCollins; Kotler, S. 2014. *The rise of superman*. New York: HarperCollins, page 21.

18 Kotler, S. and Wheal, J. 2017. *Stealing fire*. New York: HarperCollins; Kotler, S. 2014. *The rise of superman*. New York: HarperCollins.

19 Suzuki, D. 1991. *An Introduction to Zen Buddhism*. New York: Grove Press.

20 Ann, J. 2013. What I learned from a minimalist mindset. *Huffington Post*. At https://www.huffingtonpost.com/jessica-ann/what-i-learned-from-a-minimalist_b_3767628.html

21 Csikszentmihalyi, M. 1990. *Flow: The psychology of optimal experience*. New York: HarperCollins Publishers.

22 Kahneman, D. 2011. *Thinking, fast and slow*. London: Penguin Books.

23 Kahneman, D. 2011. *Thinking, fast and slow*. London: Penguin Books, page 13.

24 Kahneman, D. 2011. *Thinking, fast and slow*. London: Penguin Books, page 41.

25 Kownatzki, M., Walter, J., Floyd, S. and Lechner, C. 2012. Corporate control and the speed of strategic business unit decision making. *Academy of Management Journal*, 56(5), 1295–1324.

26 Stalk, G. 1988. Time – the next source of competitive advantage. *Harvard Business Review*, July. At https://hbr.org/1988/07/time-the-next-source-of-competitive-advantage

27 Stalk G. 1998. The time paradigm. *Forbes*, November 30, page 213–214.

28 Stone and Sand. 2014. *101 Zen stories*. At http://www.101zenstories.org/the-taste-of-banzos-sword/

29 At https://www.napoleon-series.org/research/napoleon/PopularHistory/Book2/c_popularbook2chapter1.html

30 Davis, J. and Atkinson, T. 2010. Need speed? Slow down. *Harvard Business Review*, May, page 30.

31 Davis, J. and Atkinson, T. 2010. Need speed? Slow down. *Harvard Business Review*, May, page 30.

32 Chang, C. and Groeneveld, R. 2018. Slowing down to speed up. McKinsey & Company. At https://www.mckinsey.com/business-functions/organization/our-insights/the-organization-blog/slowing-down-to-speed-up

CHAPTER TEN

About managing my many lives

SUBTEXT: An interview with extreme athlete, company leader, and family man Benedikt Boehm

1. WHAT ARE THE KEY LESSONS FROM YOUR MOUNTAINEERING CAREER THAT HAVE HELPED YOU IN YOUR CAREER AS A BUSINESS MAN AND COMPANY LEADER?

One of the key lessons of my mountaineering experiences for my business career has been the lightness. Questions such as 'what do I take with me and what do I leave behind' have really influenced my way of running our company in an increasingly complex business environment. When I started at Dynafit my first major goal was stripping the company down to its core competencies – namely, making extremely light, high-quality ski touring bindings. For the first few years we worked with the credo 'develop the core before adding more'. Just like I perfected my speed climbing style in lower altitudes before moving slowly to the 8000m peaks, we perfected Dynafit's core competencies and products before extending our product range and moving into the development of new products and markets.

Another key lesson for my way of running the company has been the teamwork with my climbing partners. This teamwork had a great impact on how I collaborate with my managers and employees in the company. Our interactions are based on mutual trust, clarity, and transparency – everything must be reciprocal and mutual. I must be as open and able to take criticism from my colleagues as they are from me. Similar to when you climb in the death zone or work on major projects with individuals who are your friends, you need to have certain clarity and calibrate the diverse expectations and goals with managers and colleagues with whom you have developed strong personal relationships over the years. Being clear and honest with each other from the start helps tremendously to keep any personal conflicts in our work relationships to a minimum.

From having faced many unpredicted or unanticipated situations in the mountains in which the wrong decisions could be fatal, I have developed an inner calmness and lightness that help me to make decisions fast. The majority of these fast decisions have been critical to the success of Dynafit. Many of these fast decisions have been polarizing. Polarizing because these decisions were often about following new ways – just like going for a new climbing route or for our unconventional mountaineering style. Dynafit is based on innovation and novelty.

We have just introduced a ski touring binding at 49 grams – half the weight of a chocolate bar! But this product has seen many trials and errors in its development phase. Our work requires an acceptance for my managers and employees to be able to fail. Sometimes failing in our product developments and sometimes in our market choices; just like we have failed from time to time to reach a peak or to finish a tour within a certain time limit. By accepting to fail we challenge the status quo every day. It requires courage and resilience. From all the things that I have seen or with which I have been confronted on the mountain – from the frozen bodies to the physical and mental sufferings – I have adapted a strong resilience and patience. My resilience, patience, and calmness have helped me to lead and protect my team particularly in times of uncertainty or economic difficulties.

2. YOU WERE NEVER TOO ENTHUSIASTIC ABOUT GOING TO SCHOOL OR UNIVERSITY. IN RETROSPECT, HOW IMPORTANT WAS YOUR EDUCATION FOR YOUR CAREER AS A MOUNTAINEER AND BUSINESS MAN?

Of course at the time, I was stressed and frustrated to have to go to school because I brought home the worst grades of all siblings even though I worked harder than them. Today, when I am looking back, I am grateful to have been able to attend school, having been able to live in an environment in which education is free and of great quality. But this gratitude has only come over time, during my expeditions in countries where I saw children who did not have accessibility to education and the employment opportunities that often come with a school diploma or degree. That's when it hit you how fortunate you have been. I would recommend to anybody who intends to pursue a career as an athlete, musician, or artist to have an education that allows for an alternative career or a Plan B.

Looking back to high school and university, I must admit these years were not only about learning math and foreign languages; they were also my first experiences of suffering and learning how to be resilient and persevere. Many times I wanted to give up, and I had to fight year after year to pass the grade and move to the next. Just getting my high school diploma was a real fight.

3. WHAT DOES A REGULAR DAY LOOK LIKE IN TERMS OF YOUR TRAINING, WORK, AND FAMILY?

I run, ski, bike in a regular week between 5000–10000 altitude meters. That is equal to five times up and down the Zugspitze.[1] Usually I train in the very early morning hours starting between 3.30–5am and finishing between 8–9am. I have learned that what I have not done in the morning I am not going to get done later in the afternoon or evening as I don't get out of the office or meeting until late. As I said in other chapters, these early morning hours of training are not only physical exercise for me, but also a form of clearing my head and developing new ideas for the business. My training runs are a great and very inexpensive form of research and development. Once I am back from the mountains I usually go directly to the office or to external appointments.

At work I like to be as efficient and effective as possible. In other words, making the most of my time at work, or getting things done with the least amount of time. This means learning to say NO to people and being able to clearly prioritize my responsibilities. This means also, for example, that I organize meetings only when they are absolutely necessary, and attend them personally only when my presence is absolutely required. I believe that business leaders waste too much time sitting in meetings and reunions of which half are not even necessary in the first place. My dislike for such meetings requires me to delegate many tasks and responsibilities. I have built a great team of directors and managers around me who I trust to make their own decisions in the best interest for the company. But this requires not only mutual trust but also communication, communication, communication. While this is an absolutely critical and well-known success factor, communication remains often a one-way affair or a sporadic process to be fallen back on only in emergency situations. In particular in conflicts I am often surprised how hard it is even for experienced managers to simply pick up the phone and to clear the air with the other party. We tend to avoid direct communication in cases of disagreements even though it is the most professional und often most successful way to deal with such situation.

Trust and delegation is also critical when it comes to organizing my family life. Even though I organize my training in a way that it interferes as little as possible with my family life, much depends on arranging the tasks and day to day activities with my wife ahead of time– and most importantly stick to what we agree on. For example, at weekends, I agree with my wife to be home by 11am regardless of however long my training session is planned for that day. The longer the training will take, the earlier I start. Thus, that is why I often get up at 2 or 3am in the morning to ensure to be back on time. And once home and done with my training, I am fully there for the family, no phone, no laptop, no disruptions from work. On normal weekdays, when I am not traveling, I get home around 7pm. That allows me to have dinner with the kids or at least bring them to bed.

Overall, my different lives – family, sport, and work (in alphabetical order) – are somewhat fluent and often one merges with the other. Training can take place when crossing the mountains on a trip to an external appointment, or the family joins me in the mountains after a training session at the weekend. My wife and I often joke that we would probably be already divorced if we were seeing each other more than we do. I understand that my way of living my lives is not everybody's version or idea of work–life balance. But then it is also not everybody's goal to climb up an 8000m mountain and ski down.

4. HOW DOES THIS AGENDA CHANGE WHEN YOU TRAIN FOR EXPEDITIONS?

There are hardly any changes in terms of the amount of training. Even before expeditions or speed mountaineering tours I hardly train more. The only thing that changes is the intensity. When I have a clear goal in sight then I often push harder, go more often to the limit, work more with harder intervals. This is critical to train my mental toughness and resilience. Because it is this mental toughness and willpower which decides if I make it to the summit and back.

5. MUCH OF THE SUCCESS OF YOUR EXPEDITIONS IS DUE TO MENTAL STRENGTH OR WILLPOWER AND SELF-CONTROL. HOW MUCH OF YOUR TRAINING IS SPECIFICALLY FOCUSING ON MENTAL ASPECTS?

People are always surprised to hear that I have never done any mental training. In particular as I have been talking on numerous occasions in this book about willpower, mental strength, and resilience. As mentioned in my response to the previous question, my mental training comes with the physical exercising and the physical suffering. And I guess what has helped me in all these years in terms of mental strength has been my growing up with great coaches who taught me to never give up a race. When you decide to start a race then you finish it.

6. HOW HAVE THE BIRTH OF YOUR CHILDREN AND YOUR FAMILY LIFE CHANGED YOUR APPROACH TO SPEED MOUNTAINEERING AND YOUR OTHER PROJECTS?

My risk aversion had already gone up before I started to have a family. I have seen so many accidents and fatal incidents over the years that I reduced all risks to a minimum – way before I got married and had my first child. I know that in my very early days of mountaineering I had pushed my luck to the limit; I often put myself into the worst kind of situations – situations which were of great risk to me and my peers without us even being aware of the risk. Thus, I am not sure if I have much luck left.

And of course most mountaineering at high altitude has some risks for which you cannot control. When the kids came I had to select tours and expeditions with the least amount of such uncontrollable risks. As a result, the K2 was no longer an option. For me the K2 and its 'bottle neck' shaped couloir overhung by glacial ice 400m below the summit are just too unpredictable. Aside giving up some of the big mountaineering goals from adolescence, much of my self-centric lifestyle died. Before it was mostly about me and my mountaineering goals; and suddenly you realize you have this responsibility for others. And that took away some of the lightness with which I got into my expeditions and tours. But these totally new experiences opened up new perspectives and ways to look at my life and what matters to me – and for this opportunity I am very grateful.

7. THERE SEEMS TO BE A TREND OF PURISM AND REDUCTIONISM WITHIN MOUNTAINEERING SPORTS. FREE SOLOING, SPEED MOUNTAINEERING, AND ALPINE MOUNTAINEERING HAVE BECOME MORE POPULAR. PHRASES SUCH AS 'LESS IS MORE' HAVE BECOME TRENDY SLOGANS. HOW DO YOU REACT AS A LEADER OF A MOUNTAINEERING EQUIPMENT COMPANY TO THIS TREND?

It is not just a trend for us; this is what we believe in at Dynafit! Our goal was always to create a product out of a little bit more than nothing. With simplicity or a certain lightness in design, and speed as its function. If any of these attributes are missing then it will not be a Dynafit product. Of course, some would argue that consumers with this 'less is more' attitude might be bad for business. As the slogan indicates they might buy fewer products. But I believe that this 'less is more' is about the functioning and handling of a product. It is much harder to simplify the design and functioning of a complex product like a ski binding than just to add a couple of functions. For us, less is more means investing enormously in research and development, in innovation and creativity, to provide the consumer with a product with a minimum of handling and a maximum of functions. This implies that our products are of very high quality that justifies our above market prices. Our brand promise is light and fast in everything we do.

8. WHAT ARE THE ROLES OF COMPANIES AND CONSUMERS ENGAGED IN OUTDOOR ACTIVITIES AND THEIR RESPONSIBILITIES WHEN IT COMES TO THE SUSTENANCE OF THE ENVIRONMENT AND THE COMMUNITIES IN WHICH THESE ACTIVITIES TAKE PLACE?

As an outdoor company we have naturally a great interest in creating environmental consciousness amongst our employees and consumers. Our philosophy of 'using a little more than nothing' and our focus on lightness implies that we use as few natural resources as possible. In our product development we are very critical about what resources we use.

Most of our products are produced close by here in Europe. Fair working conditions according to European standards and short delivery routes from our producers ensuring relatively low CO_2 emissions. Of course we have discussed to outsource some of our hardware production to Asia. But we believe that we have a social responsibility at Dynafit. And this responsibility has influenced our decision to get some of the production done in sheltered workshops in Germany where persons with disabilities assemble our ski bindings. One of the key criteria for me and our company is to produce where our products are bought and used – and that is still the Alps.

But of course there are many things which I am still not happy about – our packaging is often done with plastic based materials. We tried packaging with recyclable materials and reduced it to the minimum. But we realized that in the past many consumers were less attracted by our products. It is a moral balancing act. The recent and increasing consumer awareness of plastic waste has encouraged us to continue to push for solutions to these challenges.

9. HAVE YOUR PERSONAL EXPERIENCES DURING YOUR EXPEDITIONS IMPACTED YOU AS A BUSINESS LEADER IN TERMS OF DEVELOPING SUSTAINABLE BUSINESS PRACTICES IN YOUR COMPANY?

Yes of course. But more so in somewhat general terms. When I saw Sherpas in 2006 walking barefoot on a glacier or putting ten plastic bags over their head before they go to sleep to protect them from the cold, then you really start thinking about the societal and economic inequalities that continue to exist in most parts of the world. Dynafit and many other outdoor companies and industry partners have initiated numerous projects for Sherpas. These initiatives have greatly changed the situation for Sherpas over the years. Today the majority of Sherpas and porters are well equipped, and their risks are covered by insurance – which is a big asset for their families.

Often I am feeling in a quandary when I see the consumerism and the mountains of rubbish that it creates; and yet I am in a business in which we are animating people to buy more products – even though our products are stripped down to only the essentials. I think companies and consumers have to work more closely together – packaging is one example; but there are many more areas that we could address more successfully in collaboration with our consumers and our partners.

For example recycling used products. I believe that in the future companies will have to take on a greater responsibility when it comes to offering end-of-usage solutions to their products. Companies cannot shy away from taking on the challenge of how products are leaving the end of their product life cycle. Again, Patagonia is leading the way with its Common Threads strategy of 5Rs.[2] And Dynafit is working hard to follow Patagonia's path. For example, right now we are working on recycling solutions for our key product, the ski boots. They are still made with a lot of plastic, and we are exploring ways for the consumer to be able to return the boots to us, and methods to reuse the plastic. This takes time because we want real environmental solution and not put forward some pseudo green marketing propositions that we frequently see in our industry.

10. AS OUTLINED IN CHAPTER 7 (ABOUT SUFFERING) IT SEEMS THAT MORE AND MORE BUSINESS MEN AND WOMEN ARE SEARCHING FOR MEANING IN THEIR LIVES OUTSIDE THEIR WORKPLACE. WHAT CAN COMPANIES DO TO MAKE THE WORKPLACE MORE MEANINGFUL OR MEANINGFUL AGAIN?

Without trying to generalize too much, companies need to realize that different generations might have different expectations. For Generation Y as a group, for example, work has become a means to an end rather than the end of all means. Companies might want to revise their current mission and values to ensure that these Millenials can find some way to better identify themselves with their workplace. At Dynafit we look for people who bring a passion for the field in which we are active – and that is the mountains. This is why our philosophy is M&M – like the chocolate sweets – only that our Ms stand for Mountain and Management. It is important for us to allow our managers and employees to integrate their passion for the outdoors in their daily work routines and schedules. This is why we are moving our headquarters from Munich to Kiefersfelden right at the foothills of the German Alps – ensuring that our employees can go skiing in their lunchbreaks or go for an early morning hike before coming to work.

But as I said before, mutual trust and communication are essential in this process – the trust from the employee that he or she can really go climbing in the lunchbreak, and trust from my side that the employee is back at the time he or she has promised. Leading by example, my directors and I are giving the company its authenticity. We take company values such as 'sweating together' literally. This authenticity gives us an advantage in attracting and retaining great new talents. We just hired a very promising engineering talent who could have earned twice as much in the automobile industry that is very present in our region. But we can provide him with a work environment and work culture where he can see his personal interests being symbiotic with his job. Where the job becomes his calling. Or as we say in German: Where the 'Beruf' becomes a 'Berufung'.

Of course, we are in a business that allows for greater employee flexibility and mobility. I am not sure a hotel manager can provide the same flexibility for his or her receptionists and allow them to go skiing for a few hours when the clients await their check out or check in. But with some creativity and a will there is a way to better accommodate employees' needs and wants. Yves Chouinard, founder of Patagonia has been an important role model for me when it comes to creating a meaningful workplace. As the title of his professional biography[3] illustrates, he was able to let his people go surfing whenever the waves were right and still get them to do a great job.

11. WHAT ARE YOUR NEXT BIG PROJECTS?

In terms of mountaineering I am working on another speed ascent of an 8000m peak in 2019. After several years of reflection and being involved in numerous other sporting projects I feel ready to go back and do what I love most. Professionally, we have launched our Dynafit 365 strategy. We want to expand beyond our winter sport activities and expand into an all year round business focusing of course on activities in the mountains.

NOTES

1 The Zugspitze (2962m) is the highest mountain in Germany and lies south of the town of Garmisch-Partenkirchen.
2 Patagonia's Common Threads strategy is to reduce, repair, reuse, recycle, and reimagine.
3 Chouinard, Y. *Let my people go surfing*. New York: Penguin Group.

INDEX

accountability 76
acknowledging failure 72
acoustic startle 55
adrenaline 55
adversity 109
agenda change 161
alcohol 129
Alderfer, C. 15
alertness 37–40, 55
Alibaba 95
aligning expectations 127–30;
    egalitarianism/trust within team
    129–30; with motivations and
    objectives 127–30; open discussions
    prior to event 128–9
altruism 95–6
Amazon 36, 74, 77
ambiguity 37; *see also* uncertainty
amygdala 54–5
analyzing failures 72–4
annihilation 91
anxiety in management 55–61; *see also*
    stress management in business
Apple 74, 93
attention to detail 35–6
attentiveness 30, 52
attribution theory 41
Auden, W.H. 2, 6
Auschwitz 112
automated behavior 39
autonomic emotional reaction 55
autotelic experience 16
avalanche 4, 67–9, 86–7
awareness of death 89–92

Bandura, Albert 19
bankruptcy 74
Barra, Mary 36
Basti *see* Haag, Sebastian
Baumgartner, Felix 57, 91, 151
Becker, Ernest 90–1
being fast 150
Bell, Charlie 90
Berns, Gregory 59
Bezos, Jeff 36, 74, 109
biofeedback training 56
biological aging 95
blaming opportunity 71
bodily reactions to fear 54–5
Bonaparte, Napoleon 152
Bonnet, Nicolas 122
boredom 125
bouncing back after failure 74–5, 114
Branson, Richard 35–6
Brin, Sergey 148
Buffet, Warren 95
bulletproof CEOs 60
bureaucratic sclerosis 147
Burning Man Festival 148
burnout 107
business uncertainty 33

Campbell Soup Company 93
Campos, Tim 76–7
Cannon, Walter 55–6
cardiovascular mortality 90
Casoli, Francesco 110
Castagna, Cristina 86
causes of fear 50–1

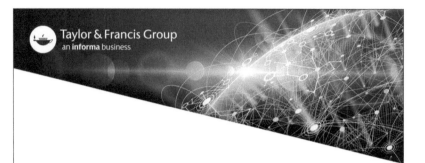